A WALK INTO PARADISE

A WALK INTO PARADISE

Burundi Sahutuga

AUDACE MPOZIRINIGA

.

CONTENTS

ACKNOWLEDGEMENTS

I AM EXPRESSING MY DEEPEST GRATITUDE TO
THOSE WHO HAVE STOOD BY MY SIDE
THROUGHOUT THIS INCREDIBLE JOURNEY OF
ENVISIONING AND CRAFTING THE
TRANSFORMED NATION OF BURUNDI
SAHUTUGA. YOUR UNWAVERING SUPPORT,
ENCOURAGEMENT, AND DEDICATION HAVE
DRIVEN THE ELABORATION OF THIS AMBITIOUS
VISION.

To my beloved wife, your steadfast love and encouragement have been my anchor throughout the challenges and triumphs of this endeavour. Your sacrifices and unwavering support have allowed me to dedicate myself to this mission.

My precious children, thank you for your understanding and patience during countless work hours. Your youthful enthusiasm, curiosity, and unshakeable faith in a better future have fueled my determination to create a transformed Burundi SAHUTUGA.

To all my partners, your collaboration, expertise, and shared vision have been instrumental in shaping the multifaceted transformation agenda. We have faced challenges head-on together, but we will celebrate countless milestones. Our collective efforts have brought us closer to realizing the dream of a prosperous and harmonious nation.

To my fellow architects: You have been the pillars of innovation, creativity, and resilience in this transformative journey. Your insights, ideas, and commitment to excellence have elevated our shared vision to new heights. Each of you has played a vital role in crafting the blueprint for Burundi SAHUTUGA.

I also extend my appreciation in advance to the countless citizens of Burundi SAHUTUGA, who will embrace this vision with open hearts and minds. Your trust and unwavering belief in the potential of our nation are a source of great motivation.

To the heroes and heroines who have fought or died for unity, democracy, and national integrity, we will forever remember you for your sacrifices. We honour your legacy by continuing the work you began.

To the international community, your support and cooperation continue to play a key role in our pursuit of peace, prosperity and global collaboration. Together, we strive to build a better world.

Finally, I offer my deepest gratitude to the Creator of the universe, who has blessed us with the wisdom and strength to embark on this transformative journey. May our efforts reflect the goodness and potential you have instilled in us.

As we move forward on this transformative path, let us continue to work hand in hand, nurturing our shared dream of a peaceful, prosperous, and united Burundi SAHUTUGA. Together, we will build a legacy that future generations will cherish.

With humility and profound appreciation,
A M

PREFACE

In the heart of Africa, a nation is crossing over tumultuous terrain, navigating the turbulent waters of division and conflicts. This nation is Burundi. As we embark on this literary journey, "A Walk into Paradise, Burundi SAHUTUGA," we must reflect on the reasons that compelled us to pen these words.

For too long, our beloved Burundi has grappled with a painful past—a history marred by division, ethnic conflicts, and mass killing. The scars of civil wars and political unrest ran deep, threatening to overshadow our land's inherent beauty and our people's resilience. The need for change was not merely a desire but an imperative.

This book is born out of necessity, from the profound belief that words can heal, unite, and transform. Our solemn conviction is that the story of Burundi, its struggles, aspirations, and unwavering spirit deserve to be etched onto the pages of history.

The necessity to write this book emerges from a troubled past, where division and conflicts repeatedly cast long and dark shadows over the nation and our beloved ones being killed without intervention. Burundi has endured periods of civil strife, a history marred by discord, and a legacy of division that threatens to define its destiny. These historical pages give us the momentum to share a vision of a united, harmonious, and prosperous nation.

In our quest to reimagine the future of Burundi, we realized that the power of transformation lies not just in the hands of a few but in the collective consciousness of its citizens. This book is an invitation, a call to action, and a testament to the unyielding hope that permeates our beloved nation. It is a mosaic of voices, experiences, and dreams woven together to create a tapestry of unity and peace.

As architects of our destiny, we recognized that a new narrative was necessary—one that transcends divisions and embraces a shared identity. We hope to provide a beacon of light that guides us away from the shadows of the past and towards the promise of a brighter future.

This book is dedicated to the citizens of Burundi, those who have endured, those who have aspired, and those who believe in the transformative power of unity and reconciliation. It is a testament to the strength of a nation that refuses to be defined by its history but instead chooses to be inspired by its potential.

As we take this "Walk into Paradise," we invite you, dear reader, to join us on this journey of discovery, healing, and renewal.

Let these words be the catalyst for a new episode in the story of Burundi —a chapter that is defined not by its past but by the boundless possibilities of its future.

With hope in our hearts and unity as our guiding star, we step forward into the pages of "A Walk into Paradise, Burundi SAHUTUGA."

INTRODUCTION

A NEW DAWN FOR BURUNDI SAHUTUGA: FROM STRIFE TO PARADISE

Welcome to the story of Burundi SAHUTUGA—a journey that encapsulates the resilience of its people, the promise of its land, and the collective determination to forge a brighter future.

In the heart of Africa, a nation will rise from the ashes of conflict and poverty to embrace a new era of transformation. In this book, we explore the evolution of Burundi SAHUTUGA from a land scarred by civil wars and economic challenges to a peaceful and prosperous paradise that we proudly call the "Paradise of Africa."

A History of Resilience:

The triumph of the human spirit over adversity marked our country's history. It is a nation that has weathered the storms of civil conflicts, overcome the barriers of poverty, and risen from the ashes more vigorously and determined. The scars of the past have become the stepping-stones towards a better future, a testament to the indomitable will of its citizens.

The Seeds of Transformation:

As architects of our nation's destiny, we recognize the need for a profound transformation. We understand that our nation's potential is more important than the challenges that held us back. We plant the seeds of change with unwavering commitment, nurturing them with unity, innovation, and steadfast determination. Through collaboration, sacrifice, and hard work, we will see those seeds bloom into a paradise that stands as a beacon of hope for Africa and the world.

A Vision of Peace:

The scars of repeated civil wars have given way to a vision of lasting peace. Burundi SAHUTUGA will become a nation where the harmonious rhythms of progress will replace the echoes of conflict. By building solid institutions, promoting dialogue, and embracing diversity, we will have woven the fabric of peace that unites us all. Our commitment to peace is unwavering, fueled by the collective understanding that it is the foundation upon which prosperity will grow.

Prosperity Takes Root:

From the fertile fields of our transformed land to the thriving industries that line our cities, prosperity will take root in every corner of Burundi SAHUTUGA. Through innovative agricultural practices, cutting-edge technologies, and strategic partnerships, we will harness the potential of our land to yield bountiful harvests and support a thriving economy. The chains of poverty will lose our transformed country, and limitless possibilities will appear ahead.

A Paradise of Progress:

Burundi SAHUTUGA's transformation is about rebuilding infrastructure and fostering a sense of community, belonging, and shared destiny—our journey from conflict to paradise is rooted in the belief that we are all architects of our future.

Through unity, inclusivity, and unwavering dedication, we create a nation that will shine as a beacon of progress—a paradise that the entire African continent can look to.

The components of **SAHUTUGA**—**SA** for Sangwabutaka (Twa), **HU** for Hutu, **TU** for Tutsi, and **GA** for Ganwa—represent the threads that have woven our history. They embody the collective strength of our past while pointing toward a united future. Each letter is a tribute to the unique identities that have shaped our society, a testament to the bonds that tie us together as citizens of this great nation.

Conclusion: A New Chapter Unfolds

As we turn the page to a new chapter in our history, we reflect on the arduous journey that has brought us to this point. Burundi SAHUTUGA is a nation transformed, a testament to the power of unity, determination, and a shared vision of prosperity. From the ashes of our past, we have forged a paradise that will stand as a testament to what we can achieve when a nation comes together with purpose and hope. Welcome to the new era of Burundi SAHUTUGA—a paradise reborn, a dream realized, and a future defined by the unwavering spirit of its citizens.

CHAPTER 1

A REFLECTION ON THE PAST

THE ROAD TO TRANSFORMATION BEGINS WITH A DEEP AND HONEST REFLECTION ON OUR NATION'S CHALLENGES. BURUNDI, ONCE MARRED BY REPEATED CIVIL CONFLICTS AND TRAPPED IN THE CYCLE OF POVERTY, FOUND ITSELF AT A CROSSROADS. THE LEGACY OF DIVISION, ROOTED IN THE MANIPULATION OF IDENTITIES, HAD SOWN THE SEEDS OF HATRED AND DISCORD. WE NEED TO ERADICATE THAT LEGACY FOR OUR NATION TO THRIVE.

The transformation of Burundi SAHUTUGA began with a brave examination of the deep-seated issues that is holding the nation back. The divisive notions of identity, rooted in historical misconceptions, had fueled conflict, hatred, and bloodshed. Recognizing this toxic foundation catalyzed change—a pivotal moment when the citizens collectively decided to redefine their narrative.

Dynamic Social Structures in the Great Lakes Region

In the context of understanding Hutu and Tutsi identities, it's essential to delve into the historical dynamics of the Great Lakes region. Contrary to the fixed tribal categories often assumed, this chapter will explore how the social structures of the area were far more fluid, allowing individuals to transition between Hutu and Tutsi categories based on economic, social, and political factors.

Fluid Identity in Pre-Colonial Times

Before colonial influence, societies in the Great Lakes region exhibited dynamic social structures that challenged rigid ethnic categorizations. Historians and researchers did not initially define the concepts of Hutu and Tutsi along strictly ethnic lines but referred them to roles within the community, economic activities, and social interactions.

The Evolution of Ethnic Labels in the Great Lakes Region: A Linguistic Exploration

Linguistic shifts, historical events, and cultural transformations have played integral roles in shaping the meanings of words and labels, particularly in the context of ethnic identities. One captivating aspect of this linguistic evolution is the origin of the terms "Hutu" and "Tutsi" in the Great Lakes Region of Africa.

The term "Hutu" is suggested to have originated from "umu-Hutu," meaning "give him this small portion," reflecting an association with concepts related to sharing or portions.

On the other hand, "Tutsi" is theorized to come from "umu-Tunzi," meaning "rich," connecting the Tutsi identity to prosperity due to their historical association with cattle herding.

It is important to note that an individual could change their status from Hutu to Tutsi and vice versa, highlighting the fluid nature of these social classifications. This fluidity adds complexity to the understanding of these terms, underscoring the dynamic interplay between language, culture, and the historical circumstances that have shaped the identities of these communities in the Great Lakes Region over time.

Social Mobility Through Economic Success

Economic prosperity shaped an individual's identity in pre-colonial times. Those who accumulated wealth through cattle herding and trade could transition from Hutu to Tutsi, irrespective of their initial background. This fluidity challenged the notion of fixed tribal affiliations and underscored the economic foundation of identity transitions.

Marriage as a Catalyst for Change

Marriage was a significant avenue through which individuals could change their identity. Intermarriage between Hutu and Tutsi families was commonplace and often led to a shift in social status. Ties formed through marriage brought about individual identity changes and fostered more significant connections and understanding between these groups.

Political Alliances and Social Status

Political alliances and affiliations also facilitated transitions between Hutu and Tutsi identities. Individuals who aligned with influential figures or demonstrated leadership qualities could ascend to Tutsi status, regardless of their origins. This malleability reflected the pragmatism of social structures in the region.

Colonial Influence and Solidification of Identities

The fluidity of Hutu and Tutsi identities began to shift under Belgian colonial rule. The colonizers introduced physical markers like height and facial features to delineate these categories, laying the groundwork for more rigid distinctions. This transformation paved the way for the perceptions of Hutu and Tutsi as fixed ethnic tribes

Legacy of Fluidity in Modern Times

Despite the colonial efforts to solidify identities, vestiges of the region's fluid social structures persisted. Memories of intermarriage, economic success, and political maneuvering continued to influence individual and collective identities. This legacy has implications for the modern understanding of Hutu and Tutsi dynamics.

Mamdani's Insights

Professor Mahmood Mamdani's research (Ph.D., Harvard, 1974) highlights the importance of considering the historical fluidity of Hutu and Tutsi identities. His work challenges the over-simplified tribal narrative and emphasizes that identities were mutable, reflecting the socio-economic and political realities of the time.

Relevance for Contemporary Context

Understanding the dynamic nature of Hutu and Tutsi identities has significant implications for the region's reconciliation efforts and conflict resolution. Acknowledging the historical fluidity can provide a more nuanced framework for addressing historical grievances and promoting peaceful coexistence.

Economic success, marriage, and political alliances influenced the social structures in the Great Lakes region by a fluidity that allowed individuals to transition between Hutu and Tutsi identities based on the factors above. This chapter has shed light on the complexities of identity in the region, challenging rigid tribal classifications and emphasizing the historical context that shaped these identities.

Burundi from its early history until its independence in 1962

Early History:

The land of Burundi has a long history of human habitation dating back thousands of years. Bantu-speaking groups began migrating into the area around the 14th century, establishing various kingdoms and chiefdoms. The Twa, a Pygmy (Abasang-wabutaka) people, were also in the region. In the 17th century, the Kingdom of Burundi emerged as a powerful monarchy. The kingdom expanded its territory and developed a hierarchical social structure with the Tutsi as the ruling class and the Hutu as the majority ethnic group. The king, known as Mwami, held significant power.

Colonial Rule

Burundi and Rwanda came under German colonial rule in the late 19th century. Following Germany's defeat in World War I, Burundi and Rwanda were placed under Belgian administration under a League of Nations mandate. The Belgians ruled indirectly, maintaining the existing social structure, and reinforcing divisions between the Hutu and Tutsi.

Independence Struggle

In the mid-20th century, Burundi witnessed growing calls for independence and political reform. The Union for National Progress (UPRONA), led by Prince Louis Rwagasore, emerged as a prominent political party advocating national autonomy. On October 13, 1961, Rwagasore, the Prince, was assassinated, but UPRONA continued its push for self-rule.

Independence

On July 1, 1962, Burundi gained independence from Belgium. The country became a constitutional monarchy with Mwami Mwambutsa IV as its king. UPRONA won the most seats in the first parliamentary elections held after independence.

However, tensions between the Hutu and Tutsi persisted, leading to sporadic violence and political instability in the years following independence. These tensions eventually escalated into full-scale ethnic conflicts and political crises in later years.

Burundi's history from its independence in 1962 up to the present:

Independence and Post-Independence Period (1960s-1970s): Burundi gained independence from Belgian colonial rule on July 1, 1962. Political instability, ethnic tensions, and a struggle for power between the Tutsi and Hutu populations marked the post-independence period. Hutu-led coup attempts and Tutsi-dominated governments led to cycles of violence and repression.

The 1965 Civil War: This conflict took place shortly after Burundi's independence. It was sparked by tensions between the Hutu and Tutsi ethnic groups over political power. The Tutsi-dominated government faced a coup attempt by Hutu military officers. The Tutsi-dominated military subsequently launched reprisals, resulting in significant casualties.

First Republic: In 1966, a coup led by Michel Micombero resulted in the overthrow of the monarchy and the establishment of a republic. The First Republic could not manage political violence, human rights abuses, and economic challenges. Ethnic tensions between Hutu and Tutsi persisted.

The 1972 Civil War: The 1972 Civil War, also known as the "Hutu Revolution," was a tragic and brutal conflict between the ethnic Hutu majority and the Tutsi minority in Burundi. It began when Hutu extremists staged a coup, leading to violence and mass killings. Thousands of Tutsi individuals, including civilians, were systematically targeted and killed, marking a dark chapter in Burundi's history. This major conflict resulted in the killing of many Hutu intellectuals and political leaders by the Tutsi-dominated military. The conflict exacerbated ethnic tensions and had a lasting impact on the nation's political and social landscape.

Second Republic: In 1976, Jean-Baptist came to power through a military coup. It's important to note that Bagaza's rule was a mix of efforts to modernize the country's economy and maintain political control. However, his authoritarian style of governance and limited political freedoms contributed to underlying tensions. He ruled the country until 1987.

Third Republic (1987-1993): In 1987, a military coup brought Major Pierre Buyoya to power. His rule initially led to some political stability and economic growth. However, ethnic tensions remained, and demands for democratic reforms increased.

The 1988 Ethnic Conflict: Ethnic tensions flared again in 1988, leading to violence and conflict initiated by Hutu ethnic groups seeking political and social reforms. This period resulted in a significant loss of life and displacement.

Civil War and Genocide (1990s-2000s): The assassination of Burundi's first democratically elected president, Melchior Ndadaye (a Hutu), in 1993 sparked ethnic violence and a civil war that lasted for years. The 1993 Burundian Tutsi genocide was a devastating conflict that primarily pitted the ethnic Hutu majority against the Tutsi minority. The conflict resulted in significant loss of life, displacement, and political and social instability. Efforts to mediate the clashes resulted in the Arusha Accords of 2000, which aimed to end the war and establish power-sharing arrangements.

Post-Conflict Period (2000s-2010s): The Arusha Accords paved the way for a transitional government and an eventual end to the civil war. However, sporadic violence and political tensions continued. The country held elections, and Pierre Nkurunziza, a former rebel leader, became president in 2005. Human rights concerns, suppression of political opposition, and controversial decisions marked Nkurunziza's presidency.

Political Crisis and Unrest (2015-2018): In 2015, Nkurunziza's decision to seek a controversial third term in office led to protests, a failed coup attempt, and a crackdown on dissent. The country experienced political instability and violence, leading to many deaths and refugee outflows.

Recent Years: In 2020, President Pierre Nkurunziza passed away, and President Evariste Ndayishimiye succeeded him. The new president promised to work towards reconciliation and development. However, challenges remain, including ongoing human rights concerns, economic difficulties, and the need for political reforms.

A complete list of Burundian presidents and how they came into power from 1966 to the present:
This list is important to understand Burundi's political history of instability, conflict, and transitions. The presidents are listed in order of succession:

Michel Micombero (1966-1976): Michel Micombero led a military coup in 1966, overthrowing the monarchy and becoming the first president of the Republic.

Jean-Baptiste Bagaza (1976-1987): Bagaza seized power in a coup in 1976 and ruled until 1987.

Pierre Buyoya (1987-1993): Pierre Buyoya took power in a military coup in 1987. He led the country through a period of political instability and ethnic tensions.

Melchior Ndadaye (1993): Melchior Ndadaye became the first democratically elected president in 1993. His presidency was tragically short-lived due to his assassination in the same year.

Ntaryamira (1994): Cyprien Ntaryamira succeeded Ndadaye but died in a plane crash the same year.

Sylvestre Ntibantunganya (1994-1996): Sylvestre Ntibantunganya served as interim president during a tumultuous period following the assassination of Ndadaye.

Pierre Buyoya (1996-2003): Buyoya returned to power in a coup in 1996 and ruled until 2003.

Domitien Ndayizeye (2003-2005): Domitien Ndayizeye was elected president following a transitional period.

Pierre Nkurunziza (2005-2020): Pierre Nkurunziza was elected president in 2005, marking a new chapter in Burundi's post-conflict history. His presidency was marked by controversies, including his decision to run for a third term in 2015.

Evariste Ndayishimiye (2020-present): Evariste Ndayishimiye is the current president from 2020. He took office following the sudden death of President Nkurunziza.

Please note throughout its history, Burundi has grappled with ethnic tensions, political instability, and challenges related to governance and development. The country's path to lasting peace, reconciliation, and socio-economic progress continues to be a complex journey.

CHAPTER 2

THE VIRUS OF HATRED AND DIVISION; THE WEAPON OF CONTROL

Unraveling the Myth: How Colonizers Fueled Hatred and Division Between Hutu and Tutsi

Within the history of many nations lies a haunting chapter—a tale of division and hatred that has scarred communities for generations. In the case of Hutu and Tutsi, a myth tale woven by colonizers served as a sinister tool to distinguish and manipulate the people, ultimately sowing the seeds of hatred, division, and mass killing.

The Fabrication of Distinction: The myth tale of Hutu and Tutsi began as a fabrication by colonial powers seeking to exploit existing social structures for their gain. With a ruthless agenda, they crafted a narrative that differentiated the two communities based on physical attributes such as height, nose, etc.

The colonizers planted the seeds of division by accentuating these superficial differences, creating a false hierarchy that pitted one against the other.

Seeds of Discord: As the myth tale spread, it ignited discord among the people who had coexisted harmoniously for centuries. The emerging divisions overshadowed deep-rooted bonds of friendship and kinship, leading to a sense of suspicion and distrust among the communities.

The colonizers skillfully utilized these tensions to maintain their dominance, weakening any attempts at unity.

Fostering a Cycle of Hatred: As the myth tale took hold, it fanned the flames of hate between Hutu and Tutsi. Communities that once shared traditions, customs and even intermarried now succumbed to mutual distrust and hostility.

The cycle of hatred perpetuated by the myth tale poisoned hearts and minds, leaving scars that would take generations to heal.

A Weapon of Control: The colonizers weaponized the myth tale to consolidate control over the region. By exploiting their created divisions, they strategically favoured one community over the other, stoking tensions and exacerbating existing inequalities.

In doing so, they maintained their grip on power, ensuring that any attempts at unity posed a threat to their dominance.

The Tragic Consequences: As the myth tale took root and divisions deepened, the consequences were devastating. The dark chapters of mass killings, fueled by hatred and manipulation, marred the nation's history, leaving a legacy of sorrow and grief.

Families torn apart, communities shattered, and trust broken left scars that continue to haunt the nation's collective memory.

A Journey Towards Healing: Unraveling the myth tale is challenging, as its roots have entrenched themselves deeply in the nation's psyche. However, confronting this dark history chapter is essential for healing and reconciliation.

Through truth-telling, dialogue, and empathy, the nation can dismantle the walls of division and embark on a journey toward unity and understanding.

In conclusion, the myth tale of Hutu and Tutsi, elaborated by the colonizers, remains a tragic reminder of the destructive power of division and manipulation. What began as a fabrication to serve the interests of foreign powers had far-reaching consequences, culminating in mass killings and lasting hatred.

As architects of our destiny, we must confront this painful history with courage and resolve. By seeking truth and fostering understanding, we can lay the groundwork for healing and, in doing so, reclaim our collective humanity, transcending the divisions that once tore us apart. Only through embracing our shared heritage and forging a path toward unity can we break free from the chains of the past and build a future rooted in empathy, peace, and harmony.

CHAPTER 3

THE DECEPTIVE MIRAGE

How Physical Appearance Became a Tool for Division and Manipulation

In the dark annals of history, insidious tactics of manipulation have been wielded by those seeking power and control. Among those deceitful methods was using physical appearances, such as nose shape, height, and other superficial traits, to distinguish further and manipulate citizens, ultimately fueling division and hatred.

During the colonial period in Rwanda-Urundi, the Belgian colonizers used physical characteristics such as nose, head, eye, height, and other features to categorize individuals as Hutu or Tutsi. This process was a part of the colonial policy of ethnic classification that aimed to create distinct and rigid ethnic identities for administrative control. It began in the early 20th century, shortly after Belgium took over colonial administration from Germany following World War I.

The Belgians introduced identity cards as a means of implementing this classification. These cards included the individual's name, fake ethnic type (Hutu or Tutsi), and the physical characteristics used for that program. These physical features included:

Nose and Head Size: Belgians believed that Tutsis had more "Caucasoid" features, including longer and narrower noses, compared to Hutus. This racial categorization based on facial features was highly problematic and is now widely discredited.

Height: Height was another factor considered. They also classified Tutsi as taller and slenderer, while Hutus were considered shorter and more robust.

The specific measuring instruments used for this purpose included calipers for measuring the width of the nose and other facial features, as well as rulers for measuring height. These measurements, which were recorded on identity cards, were introduced by the Belgian colonial authorities.

These physical measurements were highly arbitrary and contributed to ethnic tensions in Rwanda and Burundi by making these divisions seem more fixed and rooted in biology than they were. This colonial policy of ethnic classification, which solidified the perceived differences between Hutus and Tutsis, played a significant role in the social and political dynamics of Ruanda-Urundi and contributed to the conflicts that erupted later in these country's history.

This system of identity cards and the associated physical classifications introduced in the early to mid-20th century had a lasting impact on the region. However, it's essential to recognize that these classifications were not scientifically valid and have been widely harmful and divisive.

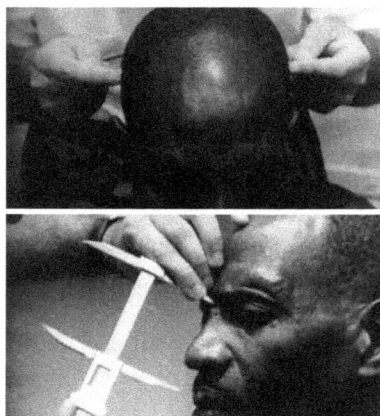

The Rwandan Myth | Sungrammata

The Impact of Using Physical Appearance

Distorting Perceptions: Using physical appearance to differentiate and categorize citizens deliberately distorts reality. The emphasis on superficial traits like nose shape and height perpetuated the notion that there were inherent differences between Hutu and Tutsi, leading to a false sense of superiority or inferiority.

Those in power manipulated perceptions by attributing exaggerated significance to these physical attributes, reinforcing divisions and sowing seeds of hate.

Seeds of Prejudice: The manipulation of physical appearance to fuel division planted seeds of prejudice among the people. The idea that one group possessed certain physical traits that made them superior or inferior fostered harmful stereotypes, deepening the chasm between communities.

This prejudiced mindset led to discrimination and further perpetuated a cycle of hostility.

Cultivating a False Hierarchy: The focus on physical appearance became a basis for creating a false social hierarchy. Colonizers used it to justify the unequal distribution of resources and opportunities, with one group being favored based on these arbitrary traits.

This artificial hierarchy perpetuated a system of oppression, keeping one community subjugated while granting privileges to another.

Those in positions of power wielded the myth of physical appearance as a weapon for control. By instilling a sense of superiority in one group and a sense of inferiority in another, they manipulated citizens to maintain their authority unchallenged.

This form of control stifled dissent and discouraged attempts at unity, ensuring the preservation of their dominance.

A Disguise for Hidden Agendas: The emphasis on physical appearance also served as a disguise for hidden agendas.

Behind the facade of distinguishing citizens based on nose shape or height lay deeper motivations of political power, economic exploitation, and cultural dominance. The diversion of physical appearance-based divisions masked the true intentions of those perpetuating this deception.

Stripping Away Humanity: Above all, the myth of physical appearance stripped away the essence of shared humanity. It dehumanized individuals, reducing them to physical traits rather than embracing the richness of their diverse backgrounds, aspirations, and dreams.

This dehumanization fueled animosity and prevented the recognition of the common bonds that united all citizens.

In conclusion, using physical appearance as a tool for division and manipulation is a dark chapter in history, highlighting the destructive power of deceit and prejudice. By distorting perceptions, cultivating false hierarchies, and dehumanizing individuals, those in power sought to control and manipulate the people for their gain.

As we reflect on this painful past, let us remember the importance of confronting falsehoods and embracing the truth. We can only move toward a future where unity, empathy, and understanding prevail by dismantling these deceptive myths and recognizing our shared humanity.

As architects of our destiny, we must strive to break free from the shackles of division and manipulation to forge a path toward reconciliation, healing, and a society where citizens' unique contributions are beyond superficial appearances. By learning from this dark history, we can aspire to build a future free from manipulation and division, where the strength of our unity prevails over the weakness of deceit.

CHAPTER 4

THE PAWNS OF
POWER

How Some Political Leaders Continued the Strategy of Dividing Citizens for Their Gain

Throughout the annals of history, the pursuit of power has driven some political leaders to employ divisive tactics to maintain their control over the masses. Just as colonial powers manipulated divisions among citizens, some political leaders perpetuated the same strategy of sowing seeds of discord to serve their interests and ambitions. Here are some of the driving forces behind their agendas:

The Lust for Power: At the heart of this tale lies the insatiable lust for power. Some political leaders, driven to remain in control, harnessed the divisive tactics inherited from the past to exploit societal fault lines.

Their thirst for authority knew no bounds, and they saw no qualms in sacrificing the nation's unity for personal gain.

Exploiting Historical Grievances: Drawing from the pages of history, these leaders used long-standing historical grievances among different communities. They sought to fuel hate and distrust by resurrecting past wounds and resentments, as a divided populace was easier to manipulate and control.

Fanning the Flames of Ethnicity: In their bid to maintain a grip on power, some leaders deliberately stoked ethnic tensions. They amplified the differences between ethnic groups, instilling fear and distrust in the hearts of citizens, all to weaken any collective opposition to their rule.

By creating an "us versus them" narrative, they hoped to consolidate their support base and silence dissent.

Evading Accountability: Rather than addressing the nation's pressing concerns, these leaders employed divisive tactics as a smokescreen. By directing the focus of citizens toward inter-community conflicts, they diverted attention away from critical issues such as governance failures, corruption, and economic inequalities.

This calculated strategy allowed them to evade accountability and prolong their grip on power.

Perpetuating a Cycle of Violence: Some political leaders perpetuated a cycle of violence by exploiting divisions among citizens. They used inflammatory rhetoric and misinformation to fuel hatred and animosity, leading to outbreaks of violence and unrest, all of which conveniently justified their iron-fisted rule. In this cycle of violence, the victims were the innocent citizens caught in the crossfire.

Undermining National Unity: The most profound consequence of these divisive strategies was the erosion of national unity. A fractured society struggles to move forward cohesively, hindering progress and compromising the collective strength of the nation.

Undermining national unity weakens the society's fabric, leaving it vulnerable to further manipulation and exploitation.

In conclusion, continuing the strategy of dividing citizens for political gain by some leaders is a disheartening testament to the thirst for power. By exploiting historical grievances, fanning ethnic tensions, and diverting attention from real issues, these leaders jeopardize the nation's and its citizens' well-being.

As architects of our destiny, we must remain vigilant against such divisive tactics. By recognizing the manipulative ploys employed by power-hungry leaders, we can stand united in pursuing a society built on empathy, understanding, and cooperation.

Let us learn from past mistakes and strive for leadership that unites rather than divides—an administration that upholds the values of justice, inclusivity, and progress.
In doing so, we safeguard the future of our nation and ensure that the dark chapters of divisive history give place to a narrative of unity and collective growth.

CHAPTER 5

THE BITTER HARVEST

Consequences of a Divided People

The consequences of a divided people reverberate far and wide, leaving a landscape scarred by poverty, ignorance, and corruption in their wake. When hate and discord invade a nation, its citizens bear the brunt of the bitter harvest of division.

Poverty and Desperation: A divided nation is often plagued by poverty, as people in power mismanage resources and opportunities squandered in pursuing power and control. The scars of historical conflicts and divisive policies hinder economic progress, perpetuating a cycle of poverty that engulfs countless lives.

Without a unified vision for progress, citizens struggle to break free from poverty and find themselves trapped in the quagmire of deprivation.

Uneducated and Uncivilized Citizens: The consequences of division extend to education and societal development. When discord replaces unity, schooling usually takes a backseat to political agendas, leaving citizens ill-equipped to face the challenges of the modern world.

An uneducated populace perpetuates ignorance and intolerance, further widening the chasm between communities and hindering societal progress.

Leaders Without Vision: Leaders often prioritize self-interest and political survival over a collective vision for the future in a nation fractured by division. This absence of visionary leadership stifles innovation and progress, leaving citizens without a clear path forward.

Leaders driven by short-term gains need more foresight to navigate complex challenges, and their leadership becomes a stumbling block to national growth.

Corruption and Erosion of Trust: Division fosters an environment ripe for corruption to flourish. As divisions deepen, trust in public institutions erodes, and those in power exploit this lack of faith to manipulate systems for personal gain.

Corruption becomes rampant, further compromising the nation's ability to address its pressing challenges and perpetuating a cycle of distrust among citizens.

Fragmented Social Fabric: The divisions among citizens fragment the social fabric that binds a nation together. Communities become insular and reluctant to engage, and communication breaks down.

This fragmented social fabric erodes the sense of a shared national identity, making it difficult for citizens to address common concerns collectively.

Stagnation and Regression: Ultimately, the consequences of a divided people manifest in the stagnation and regression of the nation, and the energy for collective progress dissipates in internal conflicts and divisive pursuits.

The nation is locked in a regression cycle, unable to break free from the chains of division and discord.

In conclusion, the consequences of a divided people are profound and far-reaching, affecting every aspect of a nation's existence. Poverty, ignorance, and corruption weigh heavily on the shoulders of citizens, while a lack of visionary leadership hinders progress and unity.

As architects of our destiny, we must recognize that the journey toward progress and prosperity begins with bridging the divides that separate us. By fostering empathy, understanding, and a collective vision for the future, we can heal the wounds of division and forge a path toward a more inclusive and prosperous society.

Only by uniting our strengths and aspirations can we break free from the shackles of the bitter harvest of division and build a nation where the well-being of all citizens is at the forefront of its priorities. Let us strive for a future where our collective potential manifests and a narrative of unity replaces the legacy of division.

CHAPTER 6

WEEDS IN A FIELD COMPARED TO HATRED IN PEOPLE"S MINDS

Weeds in a field and hatred in people's minds share intriguing parallels, offering valuable insights into the nature of both. Let's explore this comparison:

Proliferation and Overgrowth: Weeds can remarkably increase and spread rapidly, often overtaking the cultivated plants in a field. Similarly, hatred in people's minds can grow unchecked, overpowering positive thoughts and emotions. It can consume their thinking, dominating their perceptions and interactions with others.

Persistence and Resilience: Weeds are resilient and challenging to eradicate. Even when removed, they may reemerge if not thoroughly uprooted. Similarly, hatred in people's minds can be deeply ingrained, lingering even after efforts to overcome it. It may resurface during stress or conflict, necessitating constant self-awareness and management.

Choking and Hindering Growth: Weeds compete with cultivated plants for essential resources like water, sunlight, and nutrients, often blocking and hindering their growth. Similarly, hatred can stifle personal growth and hinder individuals from forming meaningful connections and experiences. It creates barriers to empathy, understanding, and compassion, preventing personal and societal development.

Spreading Contagiously: Weeds can quickly spread throughout a field, affecting neighboring areas. Similarly, hatred in one person's mind can spread contagiously, influencing those around them. Negative emotions and actions can perpetuate a cycle of hate and harm, impacting relationships and communities.

Need for Diligent Removal: Removing weeds from a field requires consistent and diligent efforts. Similarly, overcoming hatred in one's mind demands constant self-reflection, emotional intelligence, and a willingness to change negative thought patterns. It may involve seeking support from others, such as therapy or counseling.

Nurturing Positivity: To prevent weeds from taking over a field, farmers focus on nurturing and tending to the desired plants. Similarly, combating hatred in people's minds involves promoting positive emotions like love, compassion, and understanding. Fostering a mindset of empathy and kindness can help counteract the harmful effects of hatred.

Cultivating a Healthy Environment: Creating a healthy environment in a field helps minimize weed growth. Similarly, fostering a supportive and inclusive environment in society can mitigate the development of hatred in people's minds. Promoting tolerance, respect, and open dialogue cultivates a culture that discourages hatred and fosters unity.

Long-Term Prevention: Preventing weeds from taking over a field requires ongoing vigilance and proactive measures. Similarly, preventing the growth of hatred in society necessitates long-term efforts, such as education, addressing root causes of conflicts, and promoting understanding between different groups.

In conclusion, the comparison between weeds in a field and hatred in people's minds reveals the invasive and detrimental nature of both. However, as diligent cultivation and nurturing can restore a healthy plantation, addressing hate in individuals' minds requires persistent self-awareness, empathy, and a commitment to fostering a culture of understanding and compassion. By recognizing the parallels between these two phenomena, we gain insights into tending to our thoughts and emotions, promoting positive attitudes, and sowing seeds of empathy and love to cultivate a more harmonious and compassionate world.

CHAPTER 7

THE TRANSFORMATION PROCESS

7-1 Comparing the Process of Developing a Vaccine and Rebuilding a Country

Comparing the process of developing a vaccine to eradicate a virus with the rebuilding of a ruined country offers exciting parallels. Both endeavors involve a transformation journey, requiring meticulous planning, dedication, and collaboration to succeed. Let's explore this comparison in more depth:

Identify the Problem: In both cases, the first step is to identify the root cause of the issue. For vaccine development, it is crucial to understand the virus responsible for the disease and its impact on public health. Similarly, for a ruined country, an assessment of the underlying issues and challenges that led to its downfall is essential to formulate an effective strategy for rebuilding.

Develop a Plan: Just as scientists design a vaccine based on the virus's antigens, rebuilding a ruined country requires a comprehensive plan. This plan should address various aspects, including infrastructure, economy, healthcare, education, governance, and social cohesion. A well-thought-out blueprint lays the foundation for a successful transformation.

Implementation: Developing and testing a vaccine requires rigorous research and clinical trials. Similarly, rebuilding a country demands careful implementation of the devised plan. It involves collaborative efforts from various stakeholders, including government agencies, non-governmental organizations, international partners, and the local population.

Overcoming Challenges: There are bound to be challenges and obstacles in both cases. For vaccine development, challenges may include finding the suitable antigen, ensuring safety, and navigating regulatory processes. Rebuilding a ruined country involves addressing complex issues like political instability, economic disparities, social unrest, and environmental concerns. Flexibility and adaptability are essential in overcoming these hurdles.

Public Awareness and Participation: Public awareness and participation are crucial in both endeavors. For vaccines, general understanding and acceptance are vital for successful vaccination campaigns. In rebuilding a ruined country, engaging the affected population, understanding their needs, and fostering a sense of ownership among citizens are pivotal for sustainable progress.

Long-term Commitment: Vaccine development often takes years, and rebuilding a ruined country is a multi-year or even multi-decade endeavor. Both processes require long-term commitment and dedication from all involved parties. There may need to be more than short-term fixes to achieve lasting impact.

Measuring Success: In vaccine development, efficacy in preventing the disease and its safety profile is the measure of success. For a ruined country, the quality of life, socioeconomic indicators, political stability, and overall well-being of the population is the measure of success.

Global Collaboration: Both endeavors often benefit from worldwide collaboration and support. Scientists, researchers, and organizations worldwide work together to share knowledge and resources for vaccine development. Often, rebuilding a ruined country relies on international aid, partnerships, and expertise to expedite progress.

In conclusion, developing a vaccine to eradicate a virus and rebuilding a ruined country share common themes of planning, implementation, overcoming challenges, public engagement, long-term commitment, and global collaboration. Both endeavors represent transformative journeys that aim to bring about positive change and improve the well-being of individuals and communities. Just as the development of a vaccine brings hope for disease eradication, rebuilding a ruined country offers hope for a brighter and more sustainable future.

7-2 Demolishing and Rebuilding a House vs. Untying and Tying Shoes Afresh

Demolishing and rebuilding a home vs. untying and tying shoes afresh are two analogies that people can use to illustrate the concepts of significant transformation and starting anew.

Demolishing and Rebuilding a House: Demolishing and rebuilding a house is a metaphor for a significant and comprehensive transformation. When somebody rebuilds a home, it involves tearing down the existing structure, clearing away the old and sometimes bringing new components, and making way for a fresh start. This process may be the best choice when the current structure is no longer suitable, outdated, or needs substantial improvements.

The demolition stage represents the dismantling of the old, which can be challenging and sometimes emotional, especially if the house holds sentimental value. However, it also provides an opportunity to rid the property of any faults, weaknesses, or limitations the previous structure may have had.

The rebuilding phase is an exciting opportunity for innovation and creativity. It allows the incorporation of modern design elements, improved functionality, and integration of new technologies. This transformation often results in a more robust, more aesthetically pleasing, and efficient house that better meets its occupants' needs and desires.

In the context of personal growth, demolishing and rebuilding a house symbolizes a profound transformation in one's life. It may involve leaving behind old habits, thought patterns, or relationships that no longer serve a positive purpose. By doing so, an individual can create space for new experiences, opportunities, and personal development.

Untying and Tying Shoes Afresh: Untying and tying shoes afresh is a more straightforward analogy that illustrates the idea of starting over or from scratch. When a person unties their shoes, it is an act of undoing what was previously in place. It signifies a clean slate, a moment to begin again.

In untying the shoes, the knots that once held them firmly in place are loose, allowing the individual to free their feet and remove any constraints. This act is akin to letting go of preconceived notions or restrictions that may have hindered progress or growth.

Tying shoes afresh represents the act of initiating a new beginning. The individual takes the time to lace up their shoes carefully and deliberately, ensuring a secure and comfortable fit for the next part of their journey.

As a metaphor for personal growth and self-improvement, untying and tying shoes afresh implies the willingness to

release old patterns, beliefs, or limitations that have held one back. It is an act of self-empowerment, as it signifies taking charge of one's life and setting a new course for the future. Just like untying and tying shoes afresh, it invites individuals to embrace change for new opportunities with a fresh perspective.

In summary, demolishing to rebuilding a house and untying to tying shoes afresh represent the potential for change, growth, and transformation. Whether on a grand scale like rebuilding a home or on a smaller, more personal level like tying shoes, these analogies encourage us to let go of the old and embrace the new, fostering an environment for positive change and personal development.

7-3 Unearthing the Foundations of Change

In the labyrinth of our minds lie the hidden structures of thought and belief that shape our perceptions of the world. We are the architects of our mental landscapes, constructing walls of conviction and erecting fortresses of ideology. But there are times when the foundations we laid become stumbling blocks, hindering our growth, and obstructing the path to progress.

As we embark on the journey to transform our mindset, we encounter a crucial phase: to root out, pull down, destroy, and throw down. This arduous process demands a willingness to confront our innermost biases and preconceptions, acknowledging that some beliefs may have hindered us from realizing our full potential.

To root out is to dig deep, delving into the recesses of our minds to identify the seeds of negativity and self-doubt. Like experienced gardeners, we must uproot the weeds of limiting beliefs that have taken residence within us, stunting our growth, and preventing us from embracing change. It requires courage and self-awareness to confront these entrenched thoughts, knowing that only by exposing them to the light can we begin the transformation process.

Pulling down is dismantling the mental constructs that have acted as barriers, limiting our vision, and confining us to self-imposed boundaries. We may have erected walls of fear, doubts, or past failures, preventing us from embracing new perspectives and opportunities. We liberate ourselves from self-imposed confinement with every brick we remove, opening a vast expanse of possibilities.

To destroy is to confront the damaging narratives we have internalized over time. It is acknowledging the negative self-talk that has held us back and replacing it with empowering affirmations. As we shatter these destructive patterns, we create space for new beliefs that align with our aspirations and the positive change we seek to manifest.

To throw down is to release the weight of past mistakes and the burden of perceived inadequacies. We must let go of the notion that our past actions or circumstances define us. By releasing this baggage, we free ourselves to move forward unencumbered, embracing the endless potential of the present moment.

In this transformation process, we may encounter resistance from our ego, clinging desperately to the familiar comforts of the status quo. But we persist, knowing that true growth lies beyond the comfort threshold. With each thought we unroot, each wall we dismantle, and each belief we challenge, we step closer to embracing the change we desire.

Through this phase of rooting out and pulling down, we cultivate the fertile ground for a new mindset to take root. We prepare ourselves to rebuild and replant with a foundation of positivity, self-belief, and a renewed sense of purpose.

As we navigate the complexities of this transformative journey, let us remember that change is not an instantaneous event but a continuous process of growth. With patience and perseverance, we can navigate the uncharted terrain of our minds, uprooting the weeds of doubt, tearing down the walls of limitation, destroying negative thought patterns, and casting aside the burdens of the past.

In embracing the call to root out and pull down, we discover the boundless potential within us and the liberating realization that we are the architects of our destiny. The change chapter begins here, and as we embark on this expedition of the mind, we step into a new narrative of self-discovery, empowerment, and the unwavering belief that transformation is within our grasp.

7-4 Cultivating the Garden of Unity

In the barren landscapes of hearts burdened by hatred and division lies an untapped growth potential—a potential to build and plant seeds of understanding, compassion, and unity. As we journey through the intricate web of human emotions and histories, we are confronted with the challenge of transforming minds scarred by hate and prejudice into fertile grounds for positivity and harmony.

To build is to lay the foundation of understanding, brick by brick, dismantling the barriers that have separated us for far too long. We must listen with empathy, seeking to comprehend the experiences that have shaped the perspectives of others. This process requires a willingness to step outside our comfort zones acknowledging that our understanding of the world is not the only truth.

As architects of change, we must construct bridges of dialogue, connecting hearts and minds with threads of open communication. The keystones of these bridges are respect and genuine curiosity, fostering an environment where diverse voices are not silenced but celebrated. In doing so, we build a pathway towards mutual understanding, nurturing a garden of unity where the seeds of reconciliation can take root.

To plant is to sow the seeds of compassion, kindness, and empathy, recognizing that growth requires nurturing and patience. These seeds may appear small and inconspicuous initially, but their potential to flourish and blossom is boundless. We must diligently water these seeds with love, understanding, and acceptance.

We acknowledge that healing the wounds of the past and transcending division cannot be achieved through a single grand gesture but through countless small acts of goodwill. In everyday interactions, the exchanges of respect and kindness, the roots of unity stretch deeper, binding us together as a shared humanity.

Like skilled gardeners, we must tend to the garden of unity with care and perseverance, especially in adversity. We must shield the tender shoots of understanding from the harsh winds of intolerance and cultivate an environment where everyone feels valued and heard.

Building a path to mutual understanding in hearts that hold a history of hatred and division requires us to look beyond surface differences and recognize the common thread that unites us all—our shared humanity. We must foster an atmosphere where individuals feel safe to express their thoughts, experiences, and emotions without fear of judgment.

In this transformative process, we must also extend compassion to ourselves, acknowledging that growth is not linear, and setbacks may occur. But we refuse to be deterred, for the seeds of unity we plant have the potential to sprout and thrive, breaking through the barriers of hate and blossoming into a garden of harmony.

As we cultivate this unity garden, we must recognize that change is not an instant transformation but a continuous journey of learning and unlearning, building, and planting. It is a collective effort where we contribute to the rich tapestry of understanding that weaves through our communities and beyond.

In embracing the challenge of sowing good seeds in hearts with a history of hatred and division, we water the roots of empathy and understanding, nurturing a legacy of unity that future generations will inherit. Together, as we tend to this garden of transformation, we create a world where compassion transcends division, understanding replaces hatred, and the seeds of unity bear the fruits of a brighter and more harmonious future.

CHAPTER 8

THE HUMAN BRAIN IS A PLAYGROUND

THE HUMAN BRAIN IS A PLAYGROUND OF IDEAS, THOUGHTS, EMOTIONS, AND CREATIVITY. IT IS A VAST AND INTRICATE LANDSCAPE WHERE NEURONS FIRE, SYNAPSES CONNECT, AND COMPLEX NEURAL NETWORKS GIVE RISE TO THE MARVELS OF HUMAN COGNITION.

In this playground of the mind, imagination runs wild as ideas leap and bound like children at play. It is a space where memories are stored, experiences analyzed, and knowledge woven into the understanding fabric.

Emotions dance and whirl like playful companions, influencing perceptions and coloring the lens through which the world appears. Love, joy, fear, sadness, and curiosity all take turns on consciousness swings, shaping our responses to the world around us.

Creativity finds its canvas here, where inspiration and innovation collide, giving birth to art, music, literature, and groundbreaking discoveries. **In this playground, the human mind becomes an artist, sculpting thoughts into reality and bringing dreams to life.**

Yet, just like a playground, the human brain has challenges and obstacles. It may have its ups and downs, with moments of confusion and uncertainty, much like navigating the twists and turns of a jungle gym.

But it is also a place of resilience and adaptability, where the brain's neuroplasticity allows it to grow, learn, and change over time. Like children on a playground, the brain explores new territories, forging new neural pathways and expanding its capacity for knowledge and understanding.

In this playground of the mind, curiosity becomes the swing that propels us higher, and learning becomes the sandbox where we dig deep into the vast treasure troves of information.

Just as children on a playground learn to share and cooperate, the human brain thrives on connection and social interactions. It seeks to understand and empathize with others, forming bonds that enrich our lives and define our humanity.

And in the vast playground of the human brain, the games of imagination and intellect intertwine, giving rise to the endless wonders of human consciousness. It is a place of infinite exploration where the quest for knowledge and understanding never ends.

Indeed, the human brain is a playground like no other—a place where the magic of thought and the complexities of emotions come together, inviting us to discover our extraordinary potential. As we play on the playground of our minds, we uncover the boundless capacity for growth, learning, and the ever-expanding horizons of the human spirit.

The human brain's remarkable adaptability empowers individuals to learn and reshape their perspectives, attitudes, and behaviors in response to new experiences and information. This cognitive flexibility enables the acquisition and assimilation of new belief systems, ideologies, and patterns of conduct. Examples such as cohabitation, tolerance, and forgiveness underscore the brain's ability to adapt to new social norms, embrace diversity, and cultivate empathy and understanding. The human brain serves as a dynamic and evolving organ, capable of continuous learning and transformation throughout an individual's life.

SAHUTUGA was chosen to be a very easy concept and exciting for the brain, acting as a catalyst for joy and fostering hope for a new beginning. The simplicity and positivity embedded in the concept stimulate the brain's reward centers, creating a sense of enthusiasm and anticipation for the transformative journey ahead.

In the grand theater of the mind, SAHUTUGA takes center stage, conducting a symphony of joy and hope. As the neurons dance to their tune, the concept becomes a transformative force, resonating with the inherent desire for unity and a better future. SAHUTUGA, in its simplicity, emerges as a powerful catalyst, unlocking joy and kindling the flame of hope in the hearts and minds of a nation on the brink of transformation.

Jerry Bergman, Ph.D., states, "The human brain has approximately 1×10^{11} neurons that interconnect with each other 1×10^{15} times (in a changing manner). All this with a weight of around 1.5 kg and a volume of 1,300 cubic centimeters. That is enough to tell us who we are: beliefs, political preferences, sports predilections, and who we fall in love with."

https://crev.info/2022/03/brain-files-logically

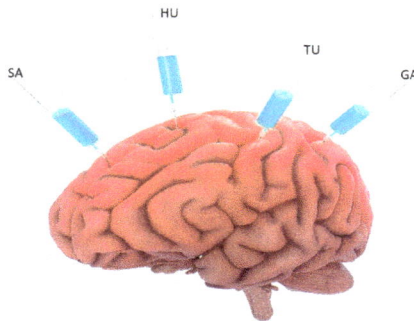

WELCOME TO BURUNDI SAHUTUGA

The phrase **"Can a country be born in a day, or a nation be brought forth in a moment?"** is a rhetorical question that challenges the idea of instant or immediate creation or transformation of a country or nation. It comes from the biblical passage in Isaiah 66:8: *"Who has ever heard of such things? Who has ever seen things like this? Can a country be born in a day, or a nation be brought forth in a moment? For as soon as Zion is in labor, she gives birth to her children."* The passage metaphorically highlights that significant and lasting changes, such as a country's birth or a nation's formation, typically take time, effort, and a development process. These transformative processes are not easily accomplished quickly but require a gradual progression, growth, and maturation.

In a broader sense, the phrase can emphasize the complexity, challenges, and complexities involved in a nation's formation, development, and stability. Building a strong, cohesive, inclusive country or nation requires careful planning, collective effort, and a long-term vision. It serves as a reminder that nation-building is a continuous process that involves multiple factors, including historical, cultural, social, and political considerations.

In a democratic country, the role of a leader in power is akin to that of a bicycle rider. A democratic leader must navigate the complex terrain of diverse opinions, just as a cyclist balances on two wheels to move forward smoothly. This analogy draws a striking parallel between leadership and the art of cycling.

Much like a bicycle with a stuck back wheel due to a lack of oil or broken bearings, constantly scraping against the road and unable to move smoothly, a leader who disregards the thoughts and needs of the people creates friction and discord within the democratic process. The collective journey toward a shared destination becomes cumbersome, hindering progress. The leader's stagnant mind, refusing to embrace the wisdom of the collective, causes delays and disappointments, leaving the people's expectations unmet.

Democratic leaders have the responsibility of steering the nation toward its collective goals. Just as the bicycle rider requires both wheels to move forward, a democratic leader needs to harness the collective wisdom and perspectives of the people to make effective decisions and lead the nation on its path to progress.

An unresponsive leader scrapes the nation's aspirations and expectations. Effective leadership requires incorporating diverse perspectives, ensuring smoother governance and alignment with the people's hopes and dreams.

A LETTER TO OUR FELLOW CITIZENS AND FRIENDS

Dear Fellow Citizens and Friends,

As the sun rises over our beloved land, its warm rays illuminate a path that beckons us toward a brighter future—an era of promise, unity, and boundless potential. With hearts brimming with nostalgia, we invite you to embark on a journey that will forever transform the narrative of our nation. The time has come to rebuild, heal, and sow the seeds of a prosperous tomorrow in the fertile soil of our collective identity.

Today we stand on the eve of a new dawn fueled by a deep yearning for change and unity. The pages of history have turned, and as architects of our destiny, we hold the pen that will script a narrative of redemption, progress, and unity.

Burundi SAHUTUGA—the name that now resonates in every corner of our land—reflects our collective transformation. It embodies our commitment to rise above manufactured divisions and embrace a shared identity transcending labels. It is a name that echoes the hopes of generations and symbolizes the unity of our purpose and the power of our collective will.

The nostalgia that tugs at our hearts is not longing for the past but for the possibilities that lie ahead. It's a nostalgia for a time when our children walk the streets without fear, our communities thrive, and our nation stands as a beacon of progress. The time to turn these aspirations into reality is now.

As citizens and friends of Burundi SAHUTUGA, the call to action is clear. It is time to roll up our sleeves, join hands, and work tirelessly to rebuild our nation. Our commitment to unity, compassion, and progress will guide us as we lay the foundations of a transformed society. Let us remember that the past does not define us, but it shapes us. And today, we stand united to shape a future that radiates hope and possibility.

We extend our hand to every citizen, inviting you to join this historic endeavor. Your voice, skills, and passion are integral to the success of our mission. Let us rally around the call to action —to rebuild our nation, cultivate harmony, and create opportunities to uplift every society member.

To our friends beyond our borders, we extend an invitation to stand with us to support our journey toward a brighter future. Your solidarity, expertise, and partnership will amplify our efforts' impact and reinforce our commitment to change.

The time is now, dear citizens and friends—the time to reclaim our nation's destiny and shape a legacy that resonates for generations. Together, let us breathe life into the dream of Burundi SAHUTUGA—a paradise of hope, progress, and shared aspirations.

In the spirit of togetherness, we extend our invitation to all of you. Join us as we embark on rebuilding, healing, and progress. Your skills, passion, and dedication are the building blocks of our transformed nation. Let us embrace the nostalgia for a time of our dreams and bring those dreams to life.

The road ahead will not be without challenges, but the strength of our unity will carry us through. Let us make history together, not through the battles of the past but through the victories of the future. The time is now, and the opportunity is ours.

With hope in our hearts and a nostalgic yearning for a better tomorrow,

Audace Mpoziriniga
Architect of the Transformed Nation
Burundi SAHUTUGA

CHAPTER 9

EMBRACING THE JOURNEY OF RENEWAL

In the quiet moments of introspection, a realization dawns upon us—the need for a change of mindset, a fresh perspective that breathes new life into our experiences. Like tying shoes afresh, we embark on the journey of initiating a new beginning —one where we take deliberate steps to ensure a secure and comfortable fit for the next part of our journey.

Untying the knots that had bound our thoughts and beliefs is to free ourselves. We gently release the constraints of the past, allowing ourselves the freedom to explore new paths and possibilities. As we unravel the tightly woven threads of old habits and patterns, we recognize that our mindset is not a stone but a canvas ready to be repainted.

With each knot untied, we let go of limiting beliefs that may have held us back. We shed the weight of self-doubt and negative self-talk, creating space for positivity and self-empowerment to thrive. We challenge the assumptions we once held dear, questioning their validity, and opening ourselves to alternative perspectives.

While tying shoes afresh, we engage in deliberate care and mindfulness. Each lace is threaded with intention, symbolizing our purposeful steps toward a positive mindset change. We approach this task patiently, understanding that transformation is a gradual process requiring consistent effort and dedication.

As we meticulously tie the knots, we find stability and security in our newfound mindset. We anchor ourselves believing we can shape our thoughts and attitudes, directing them towards growth and self-improvement. Just as well-laced shoes provide a stable foundation for the journey ahead, a well-tied mindset equips us to navigate life's challenges with resilience and grace.

Tying shoes afresh invites us to embrace the beauty of the present moment. It urges us to be fully present in the change process and to savor each step we take on this transformative path. We appreciate the journey, recognizing that growth and renewal unfold in the everyday moments of self-awareness and self-compassion.

Through this mindset change, we open ourselves to the endless possibilities that lie before us. We welcome curiosity and adaptability as companions on our journey, inviting them to guide us toward new perspectives and opportunities. We find the courage to embrace uncertainty, understanding that it is the fertile ground where personal growth takes root.

In moments of self-reflection, we celebrate the progress we have made. Just as each knot tied is a testament to our commitment to change, each tiny shift in mindset becomes a stepping stone toward personal transformation. We acknowledge that every step forward, no matter how small, leads us closer to the person we aspire to become.

Tying shoes afresh is not a singular event but a lifelong practice. As we journey through the ever-changing landscapes of life, we embrace the fluidity of growth, welcoming each twist and turn with an open heart. We honor the essence of this transformative journey, recognizing that it is not about reaching a destination but about embracing the continuous process of self-discovery and renewal.

With our mindset securely tied, we embark on this exhilarating journey of self-evolution, eager to explore the boundless horizons of possibility that await us. Let us walk this path confidently, knowing that we have the power to shape our mindset and, in doing so, shape our lives' trajectory.

CHAPTER 10

TOWARD A DEMOCRATIC FUTURE

Transitional Democracy

Transitional democracy is a governance system designed explicitly for post-conflict situations. It focuses on rebuilding democratic institutions, establishing the rule of law, protecting human rights, and fostering reconciliation. Transitional democracies often emphasize national unity, peacebuilding, and transitional justice mechanisms to address past grievances.

10-1 A Bridge to Democracy: The Power of a United Transitional Government

In the quest to bridge a nation to a democratic system, forming a united Transitional Government stands as a beacon of hope. Drawing upon the collective strength of political parties in opposition and power, alongside other essential groups such as non-governmental organizations (NGOs) and diaspora representatives, this alliance holds the potential to pave the way for a democratic future founded on indivisible, transformed families.

A Confluence of Perspectives: A Transitional Government forged from diverse political parties represents a confluence of perspectives. By bringing together voices from both opposition and ruling parties, the government transcends partisan interests and focuses on the nation's greater good.

This amalgamation of ideas fosters dialogue and inclusivity, enabling the formation of comprehensive policies that address the needs of all citizens.

The Crucial Role of NGOs: Non-governmental organizations play a vital role in the transitional process. As independent actors dedicated to improving society, they bring valuable expertise and insights.

Their engagement ensures that the government remains accountable to the people and that policies are within the interests of the marginalized and underrepresented.

Diaspora Representation: Including diaspora representatives in the Transitional Government strengthens the connection between the nation and its global community. Diaspora members bring diverse experiences and perspectives, often serving as bridges to international networks and resources.

Their involvement fosters a sense of unity between citizens at home and those abroad, making the nation's transformation a collective endeavor.

A Solid Platform of Transformed Families: At the heart of this united Transitional Government is the vision of a nation founded on transformed families. These families, liberated from the chains of division and conflict, serve as the bedrock for a cohesive and harmonious society.

By prioritizing the well-being and prosperity of families, the government sets in motion a virtuous cycle of progress that extends from households to the entire nation.

A Journey to Democratic Values: The Transitional Government's mandate revolves around fostering democratic values such as accountability, transparency, and participatory governance. Embodying these principles, the government sets an example for the nation's future democratic institutions.

This journey towards democracy is not a swift process but a meticulous endeavor that demands commitment and perseverance from all stakeholders.

A Collective Responsibility: The success of the Transitional Government relies on the collective responsibility of all involved. Political parties must set aside short-term gains and work collaboratively for the greater good.

NGOs should continue their advocacy for social justice and equality, while diaspora representatives must bring forth the perspectives of their global communities.

In conclusion, a united Transitional Government comprised of political parties, NGOs, and diaspora representatives is a potent force in paving the way for a democratic system founded on transformed families. Through inclusivity, dialogue, and accountability, this alliance of diverse perspectives can chart a course toward a future where the well-being of citizens remains paramount.

As architects of our destiny, we must recognize the significance of this collective endeavor. Together, hand in hand, heart to heart, let us embark on this journey of transformation and democracy, guided by the conviction that a united and harmonious nation is within our reach. **By building bridges between opposing factions and embracing the power of diversity, we can lay the foundation for a democratic society where every citizen's voice is valued and the dreams of transformed families flourish.**

10-2 The Power of Transformed Identity, Family Tree, and Nation's Family Name

In the trajectory of progress, the transformation of identity, family tree, and a nation's family name serves as a powerful catalyst toward establishing a democratic system. As citizens embark on a journey of self-discovery, collective healing, and unity, they pave the way for a future where democratic ideals can flourish, and the voices of the people can shape the course of their nation.

'

A Transformed Identity: At the heart of a democratic system lies the recognition of individual agency and the right to self-determination. As citizens transform their identity, shedding the confines of historical divisions and embracing a sense of shared humanity, they lay the foundation for a democratic society. A transformed identity breaks down the barriers that once separated citizens, fostering a spirit of inclusivity and openness to diverse perspectives.

In this democratic transition, each citizen's voice is recognized and valued, regardless of background or societal status. The identity transformation empowers citizens to engage in civic life actively, contribute to the nation's discourse, and actively shape the future they envision.

A Transformed Family Tree: A democratic society thrives on the principles of unity and cooperation, where diverse voices come together to seek common ground. The transformation of the family tree is an integral part of this process. As families embrace empathy, understanding, respect, and forgiveness, they become microcosms of democratic ideals, where open dialogue and consensus-building are practiced.

The values cultivated within the transformed family tree, which are compassion, justice, and fairness nurture future citizens who are invested in the welfare of their communities. These future citizens carry the legacy of a transformed family tree into the public sphere, becoming advocates for social equity and agents of positive change.

A Transformed Nation's Name: Renaming a nation to reflect unity in diversity symbolizes a nation's commitment to a democratic future. By acknowledging past divisions and embracing a shared identity, the country symbolizes its dedication to building a society where the voices of all citizens matter.

A transformed nation's name becomes a unifying force, transcending tribal affiliations and historic labels. It embodies the principle that every citizen has an equal stake in the nation's trajectory and that their perspectives and aspirations should be heard and considered in the democratic process.

As the transformed nation's name becomes a beacon of hope for future generations, it inspires citizens to participate in the democratic process. Citizens are encouraged to vote, engage with their elected representatives, and participate in civic activities that promote social welfare and justice.

The Democratic Transition: The transformation of identity, family tree, and a nation's name sets the stage for a smooth and successful transition to a democratic system. As citizens embrace the values of empathy, inclusivity, and respect, they are more likely to foster democratic practices such as dialogue, compromise, and mutual understanding.

In a democratic society, the government serves as a representation of the will of the people. **Through free and fair elections, citizens can elect leaders who reflect their values and aspirations.** The democratic transition empowers citizens to hold their leaders accountable and actively participate in their nation's decision-making processes.

Furthermore, a transformed identity, family tree, and nation's name create an environment where diverse perspectives are welcomed and valued. Democratic systems thrive on the richness of diverse opinions as they lead to more comprehensive and equitable policymaking.

In conclusion, a transformed identity, family tree, and nation's name pave the way for a democratic future. These transformative processes foster unity, healing, and a sense of collective responsibility. As citizens embrace their shared humanity, they become active participants in shaping a democratic society that upholds the principles of justice, equality, and inclusivity. The democratic transition becomes a natural progression guided by empathy, respect, and a commitment to building a more equitable world for all. As architects of our destiny, we recognize the power of these transformations in shaping a future where democracy thrives, and every citizen's voice is heard and respected.

10-3 Empowering Citizen Voices: The Democratic Transition of Identity

In the journey towards a democratic society, the transformation of identity becomes a pivotal step that empowers citizens to play an active role in shaping their nation's destiny. As the democratic transition unfolds, each citizen's voice is recognized and valued, breaking free from historical divisions and societal status constraints. The transformation of identity becomes a powerful catalyst that encourages citizens to engage in civic life actively, contribute to the nation's discourse, and shape the future they envision.

Recognition and Value of Every Citizen's Voice: In a truly democratic society, every citizen's voice carries weight and significance. The identity transformation ensures that historical divisions and social hierarchies do not limit a person's ability to participate in the democratic process. Whether from marginalized communities or privileged backgrounds, each citizen is vital to the nation's collective voice.

The democratic transition fosters an environment where citizens feel seen, heard, and acknowledged. This recognition instills a sense of belonging and responsibility, motivating citizens to actively engage in civic activities and take ownership of the nation's affairs.

Empowerment to Engage in Civic Life: The identity transformation empowers citizens to step forward from the sidelines and participate actively in the nation's life. It encourages them to go beyond mere observers and become agents of positive change.

Through the democratic transition, citizens understand that their involvement is crucial in building a society that reflects their values and aspirations. They are inspired to educate themselves about political processes, policy matters, and the issues that affect their communities. This empowerment enables citizens to make informed choices and influence decisions that shape the nation's trajectory.

Contributing to the Nation's Discourse: In a democracy, public discourse serves as the nation's heartbeat. The identity transformation invites citizens to participate in meaningful conversations and contribute their unique perspectives to the broader dialogue.

By engaging in respectful debates, citizens explore diverse viewpoints, formulating comprehensive policies that address all needs. The democratic transition encourages citizens to seek common ground and bridge differences through dialogue and understanding.

Shaping the Future: As citizens embrace their transformed identities, they become proactive architects of the nation's future. They envision a society that embodies their values of justice, equality, and inclusivity. This vision serves as a guiding compass, directing their efforts toward building a nation that reflects their aspirations.

The democratic transition ensures that no single group dominates the narrative but that the collective wisdom of all citizens shapes the nation's path. Every voice contributes to the tapestry of ideas, policy proposals, and visions that define the nation's future.

In this democratic transition, the power of identity transformation becomes evident as citizens move from passive spectators to active participants in the nation's governance. They shed the labels that once defined them narrowly and embraced their common identity as citizens united by a shared destiny.

Through the democratic transition, the nation taps into its diverse citizenry's wealth of ideas, experiences, and perspectives. This inclusivity strengthens the social fabric, fostering cohesion and resilience even in adversity.

In conclusion, the democratic identity transition marks a profound shift in a nation's trajectory. As each citizen's voice is recognized and valued, the transformation empowers them to take charge of their future. Engaging in civic life, contributing to the nation's discourse, and shaping the future they envision become inherent responsibilities for every citizen.

In a transformed society, the democratic values of representation, fairness, and inclusivity flourish. As architects of our destiny, we embrace the power of identity transformation as the foundation of a vibrant and thriving democracy. By amplifying every citizen's voice, we pave the way for a future where collective aspirations shape the nation's destiny—a future of justice, equality, and prosperity for all.

10-4 A Bridge to Stability: Integrating Combatants for Democracy

In the transformation journey of Burundi SAHUTUGA, the scars of past conflicts can only fully heal when those who once defended ideals aligning with our nation's vision find a renewed purpose. Combatants who dared and continue to demand a stable and democratic system for fair elections hold a unique potential to contribute to our unified nation. By offering them a path to integration into the national army, we forge a bridge to a more stable and democratic future.

Honoring Commitment: From Conflict to Service

For those who fought to uphold democratic principles and the integrity of the electoral process, a new opportunity awaits. Integrating former combatants into the national army recognizes their dedication to safeguarding democratic values. This transition serves as an act of acknowledging their previous commitment and channeling their energy toward the collective goal of preserving stability and promoting a solid democratic foundation.

Meeting Requirements: Upholding Excellence

Integrating former combatants into the national army must be guided by strict criteria that ensure our armed forces' integrity, effectiveness, and professionalism. These criteria go beyond past allegiances; they include rigorous assessments of skills, fitness, discipline, and aptitude. By adhering to these criteria, we build an army that is robust, capable, and committed to upholding our nation's values.

A Unified Force: Cultivating Cohesion

The integration process goes beyond technical aspects—it encompasses fostering unity within our national army. As they transition into their new roles, former combatants undergo training, orientation, and mentoring that align them with the broader objectives of our transformed nation. This cultivation of unity ensures that individuals from diverse backgrounds can work seamlessly together for the common good.

Guardians of Democracy: Protecting Progress

The presence of former combatants who once fought for democracy within our national army carries a powerful symbolism. They serve as guardians of our democratic system, reminding us of the importance of peaceful transitions, free elections, and transparent governance. Their presence stands as a reminder that the sacrifices of the past were not in vain and that the future holds promise for continued progress.

A Symbol of Hope: Renewed Purpose

Integrating former combatants into the national army reflects our commitment to offering a path of redemption, renewal, and transformation. By allowing them to serve their nation through a democratic institution, we enable them to transition from a history of conflict to a future of service. Their journey is a symbol of hope and a testament to the power of a second chance.

A Unified Future: Forging Ahead Together

In welcoming former combatants who were champions of democratic ideals into our national army, we create a unified force dedicated to preserving stability and democratic values. Their integration reminds us that our nation's transformation is a collective effort, where everyone—no matter their past—can play a pivotal role in building a brighter future.

A New Chapter: Continuation of Transformation

As Burundi SAHUTUGA continues its transformative journey, integrating former combatants into the national army is a testament to our commitment to inclusivity, reconciliation, and stability. This chapter represents an opportunity to turn the page on the past and join hands in shaping a democratic and harmonious future. By embracing those who once dared to defend our nation for
fair elections, we reinforce the foundations of our transformed society—a society built on unity, democracy, and progress.

10-5 Path to Peace: Disarmament, Demobilization, and Reintegration (DDR) of Youth Militia

In the transformative journey of Burundi SAHUTUGA, the spirit of past conflicts casts a long shadow. To secure a lasting peace and lay the foundation for a harmonious society, we recognize the crucial importance of the Disarmament, Demobilization, and Reintegration (DDR) process. This chapter delves into the strategies and principles that underpin our commitment to DDR—a vital step toward a future free from the shackles of violence.

Disarmament: Breaking the Chains of Violence

Disarming youth militia is the first step toward peace and stability. Through a carefully coordinated process, weapons that were once instruments of destruction will be safely collected and removed from our streets and communities. Disarmament is not merely collecting arms; it is unburdening our society from the weight of violence and the threat it poses to our collective well-being.

Demobilization: A Bridge to Civilian Life

The transition to civilian life can be challenging for those who have borne arms. To ensure a smooth reintegration, we commit to a comprehensive demobilization process that provides a safe passage from military to civilian life and offers psychological and emotional support. Access to counseling, trauma healing, and mental health services will form the bedrock of this phase, allowing former combatants to shed their old roles and embrace new identities as agents of peace.

Reintegration: Building New Horizons

Reintegration is more than a return to everyday life; it is an opportunity for rebirth. Youth militia will be reintegrated into society with a comprehensive approach that includes skills training and livelihood opportunities. By offering avenues to economic empowerment and personal growth, we seek to eliminate the drivers of violence and create paths to prosperity. This holistic approach addresses the root causes of conflict, fostering an environment where the allure of violence pales compared to the promise of a brighter future.

Addressing the Root Causes: A Holistic Approach

The DDR process is not confined to the mechanics of disarmament, demobilization, and reintegration. It is deeply rooted in addressing the underlying factors that fueled conflict. Burundi SAHUTUGA is committed to tackling poverty, inequality, and marginalization head-on, dismantling the structural forces perpetuating violence. By providing access to education, healthcare, and economic opportunities, we seek to create an environment where violence is rendered obsolete by the allure of progress.

Safeguarding the Future: Preventing a Return to Violence

The DDR process is not a solitary event but a continual commitment to safeguarding the future. Our nation will monitor and support the progress of reintegrated individuals, providing ongoing mentorship, guidance, and support as they navigate their new lives. In preventing a return to violence, Burundi SAHUTUGA recognizes that building sustainable alternatives is paramount to securing a peaceful future for future generations.

Unity in Transformation: A Shared Journey

The journey of DDR is not one that individuals embark upon alone—it is a shared endeavor, a collective march toward peace. The government, civil society, international partners, and, most importantly, the citizens of Burundi SAHUTUGA must work hand in hand to ensure the success of the DDR process. By providing a second chance to those who once wielded weapons, we are not merely transforming individuals but shaping our society's very fabric.

In fostering an environment of healing, growth, and opportunity, we plant the seeds of reconciliation that will blossom into a future free from violence. The DDR process is a testament to our commitment to a transformed nation that values its citizens, dismantles the vestiges of conflict, and paves the way for a future of unity, peace, and progress.

10-6 Election of Leaders

In our transformed nation, the election of leaders takes on a new meaning. Rather than being driven by divisive sectarian interests, it is guided by a shared vision for the future of Burundi SAHUTUGA. Ethnic or tribal labels do not confine our leaders; They are architects of a united, prosperous, and secure nation. Social codes such as SA, HU, TU, and GA would not cause inquietude among citizens if this concept were applied because they know they are all brethren and trust their leaders for peace, security, and prosperity.

This transformation is built on recognizing that our past divisions have only hindered our progress and brought about suffering. It is time to turn the page and embrace a new era where the national interest prevails over any other consideration.

In the SAHUTUGA concept, leaders are elected based on their commitment to national development, peace, and vision for a prosperous and harmonious future. Citizens, regardless of their background, come together to choose the individuals who will guide our nation toward a brighter tomorrow.

The focus is on policies and programs that uplift all our people, on infrastructure that connects our communities, on education that empowers our youth, and on opportunities that enrich the lives of every citizen. Once elected, our leaders represent the people's collective will to move beyond the divisions of the past.

In this vision, the old codes no longer hold sway. Instead, a new code emerges, one of unity, progress, and shared

prosperity. The citizens' trust in their leaders is no longer determined by ethnic or tribal affiliations but by their ability to lead the nation toward a future where every Burundian SAHUTUGA is proud to call this land home.

The SAHUTUGA concept is a powerful reminder that we can break free from the shackles of the past and forge a path forward as one united nation. The selection of our leaders is not a matter of 'us versus them' but an affirmation that we are all in this together. With our eyes set on a shared horizon, our leaders guide us towards a Burundi SAHUTUGA that knows no divisions, only unity.

CHAPTER 11

THE CANVAS OF MOTHERHOOD

11-1 Nurturing the Tapestry of Diversity

In the symphony of creation, a mother's womb emerges as a sacred canvas—a realm where the brushstrokes of life take shape and identities flourish. Just as a landscape harbors the potential for many plant species, a mother's womb cradles the potential for many lives. This chapter delves into the profound parallel between the nurturing power of the land and the embrace of motherhood, revealing the awe-inspiring truth that within each womb, there is a destiny of our transformed nation delicately woven.

Seeds of Life and the Blueprint of Identity In the expansive realm of nature, seeds hold the promise of countless plant species, each with its unique characteristics and beauty. In parallel, the mother's womb can contain the seeds of humanity's diverse identities—**Sangwabutaka (Twa), Hutu, Tutsi, Ganwa**, and more. Just as seeds hold the blueprint for plants, the human genetic code has the potential for individuals with distinct identities, traits, backgrounds, and destinies. Within the womb's sanctuary, the journey of these identities begins, nurtured by the mother's body and spirit.

The Nutrients of Nurturing: Diversity Thrives As a land provides nourishing nutrients to sustain various plants, a mother's body provides the nurturing environment essential for diverse lives to flourish. The mother's blood supports the embryo's growth, just as soil offers nutrients for germinating seeds. Each life nurtured within the womb is a testament to the incredible capacity of the human body—a vessel that nourishes and supports the diversity that shapes our nation's identity.

Celebrating Individuality and Unity The symphony of diversity plays out within the womb's sanctuary. Just as the different elements of a landscape come together to create a harmonious ecosystem, the unique attributes of each identity converge within the nation's embrace. The unity of our transformed nation emerges not from conformity but from the celebration of individuality—a harmony that springs forth from the recognition that each identity contributes its unique melody to the grand composition of our shared narrative.

A Tapestry Woven with Care As the mother's body carefully nurtures each developing life, our transformed nation also carefully nurtures the diverse identities that compose its fabric.

Each identity brings a story, a history, and a unique contribution that enriches the collective narrative. The weaving of this tapestry is an act of love—an affirmation that our nation finds its strength, beauty, and resilience in the tapestry of its people.

Empowering the Generations Just as seeds hold the potential to propagate future plant generations, the nurturing embrace of motherhood propels new generations of identities forward. The cycle of life continues, each identity sown with the potential to bloom into a force of progress and transformation. The mother's womb's legacy becomes our nation's legacy—a legacy that stands as a testament to the power of diversity, the spirit of unity, and the nurturing embrace of a transformed identity.

In pondering the parallel between a landscape's potential for varied plants and a mother's womb's potential for diverse identities, we uncover a profound truth—the womb's embrace is a canvas upon which the destiny of our nation is painted. Just as the landscape thrives with the coexistence of different plants, so too does our country thrive with the coexistence of diverse identities. As the mother's womb nurtures life, so does our nation nurture its various citizens—a place where individuality is cherished, unity celebrated, and the promise of a transformed identity takes root and blossoms.

As architects of our destiny, we must be open to self-discovery and self-rediscovery. Just as God's creation unfolded step by step, our understanding of self deepens with time and experience. We learn from the tapestry of our past, draw strength from our present, and envision the possibilities of our future.

11-2 Seasons of Identity: Embracing Our Destiny in Burundi SAHUTUGA

In the heart of Burundi SAHUTUGA's transformation lies a profound recognition of the power bestowed upon us by the Creator of the universe. Just as God meticulously designed each element of the cosmos, we, as citizens of this transformed nation, possess the remarkable ability to shape our destiny. Inspired by the rhythmic harmony of the seasons, we have chosen to align our identity with the months of our birth, forging a united path toward a brighter future.

The Blueprint of Creation: A Universe of Design

From the grandeur of galaxies to the intricate details of earthly life, the universe unfolds in harmonious patterns. Just as God orchestrated the symphony of creation, we find ourselves within this magnificent tapestry endowed with the capacity to enact change, growth, and evolution. This shared power connects us to the essence of our existence and empowers us to mold our nation's destiny.

A Reflection of the Divine: Embracing Our Image

As humans, created in the image of God, we carry a sacred responsibility to nurture the world around us. Just as God breathed life into us, we breathe life into Burundi SAHUTUGA's vision— unity, progress, and prosperity. Our ability to shape our identity, unbound by historical divisions, reflects the divine attribute of creation itself, a testament to our role as architects of our transformed nation.

11-3 Months of Birth: Uniting Identity and Destiny

In pursuing unity and a shared destiny, we have chosen to associate our identity with our birth months. Just as the seasons usher in change and renewal, this alignment carries a profound symbolism. **January, May, and September are linked to Sangwabutaka (Twa); February, June, and October are associated with Hutu; March, July, and November are connected to Tutsi; April, August, and December are tied to Ganwa.** Each segment of the year represents not only our diverse but harmonious identity.

CHRONOLOGICAL ORDER OF SOCIAL CODES: SAHUTUGA

January=====================**SA** (Sangwabutaka)
February====================**HU** (Hutu)
March======================**TU** (Tutsi)
April======================**GA** (Ganwa)
May========================**SA** (Sangwabutaka)
June=======================**HU** (Hutu)
July=======================**TU** (Tutsi)
August=====================**GA** (Ganwa)
September==================**SA** (Sangwabutaka)
October====================**HU** (Hutu)
November===================**TU** (Tutsi)
December===================**GA** (Ganwa)

A Holistic Nation: Components of Unity

In this orchestrated rhythm of months, our transformed nation finds cohesion. Just as each season contributes its unique elements to the environment, our identity components—**Sang-**

wabutaka, Hutu, Tutsi, and Ganwa—form the pillars of Burundi SAHUTUGA. Like the interconnected web of nature, these identities weave the fabric of a united society, fostering understanding, respect, and collaboration.

A Living Metaphor: The Changing Landscape

Just as the changing seasons transform the landscape, our approach to identity reflects a dynamic shift. This shift underscores our nation's commitment to adapt, evolve, and progress. The journey of Burundi SAHUTUGA parallels the cycles of growth and renewal found in nature, where each phase contributes to the larger narrative of development and unity.

A Destiny Defined: Architects of Change

In embracing our birth months to redefine our identity, we acknowledge the sacred privilege of shaping our destiny. This act embodies our role as stewards of a transformed nation, architects who honor our shared past while carving a path toward a unified future. Just as God's design is woven into the very fabric of our universe, our identity in Burundi SAHUTUGA reflects our commitment to the betterment of ourselves and our nation.

Unity in Diversity: A Gift and a Responsibility

With unity as our guiding light, we embrace the diversity that enriches our society. We recognize that as we harmonize our identity, we forge a destiny that transcends divisions and fosters a culture of compassion, respect, and progress. As the seasons of identity unfold in our transformed nation, may we be reminded of our profound interconnectedness and the enduring legacy we are crafting for generations to come.

11-4 Harmony in Diversity: Seeds of Unity Born in the Same Family

In the enchanting landscape of our transformed nation, the beauty of diversity blooms from the very soil we walk upon. Just as a single field nurtures a tapestry of crops, each with its unique qualities, our families thrive with a rich blend of identities. Just as beans, maize, potatoes, and cassava coexist harmoniously in a single field, so too can individuals such as Sangwabutaka, Hutu, Tutsi, and Ganwa be born into the same family. **Within the confines of a family, individuals are born with different "social codes," like Sangwabutaka, Hutu, Tutsi, or Ganwa, based on the month they were born.**

This wondrous analogy brings to light the undeniable truth that our identities are not rigid compartments, but threads woven together to create the vibrant fabric of Burundi SAHUTUGA. Our nation's soil doesn't discriminate; it offers a nurturing embrace to all born upon it, regardless of affiliation. As crops share the same earth, families share the same air, water, and history.

The rhythm of life doesn't halt for divisions, nor should our hearts. The seasons change, the sun rises, and sets, and the family bonds remain unbroken through it all. The stories whispered by the winds that rustle through the leaves carry with them the lessons of unity that have been ingrained in the very DNA of our land.

Imagine the beauty of a family gathered around a table, sharing meals, stories, and laughter. Now imagine that family composed of Sangwabutaka, Hutu, Tutsi, and Ganwa members, their diverse identities intertwining to create a

rich tapestry of experiences. Just as the crops contribute to a nourishing feast, so do our backgrounds enrich the collective narrative of our nation.

This chapter of our journey emphasizes that our identities are not separate entities, but threads woven together by the common thread of being Burundi SAHUTUGA citizens. Like plants nurtured by the same sun and rain, we share the same resources, opportunities, and responsibilities that our transformed nation offers.

Just as a field requires care and attention for its bounty to flourish, our nation requires unity and understanding to reach its full potential. As Sangwabutaka, Hutu, Tutsi, and Ganwa coexist in the same family, let us embrace the truth that our destinies are entwined as citizens of Burundi SAHUTUGA. The same sun that warms one heart warms us all, and the same rains that nourish one soul nourish us all. Let us stand united in our diversity, a living testament to the fact that in the garden of our nation, the most beautiful flowers bloom when all are given the chance to thrive.

CHAPTER 12

EMBRACING OUR DESTINY AS ARCHITECTS OF CHANGE

12-1 The Power to Shape our Life

In the heart of our nation, a profound awakening has taken root. We, the citizens, have come to realize that we hold the power to shape the course of our destiny. No longer content to be passive spectators in the grand theater of life, we have risen as architects of change, determined to craft a future that resonates with the ideals we hold dear.

With unwavering resolve, we embark on a journey that transcends personal gains and fleeting ambitions. Our vision extends far beyond the horizon, for we understand that our choices today will echo through the corridors of time, affecting generations yet to come.

We acknowledge that transformation is not an easy path, nor is it the pursuit of a solitary soul. It is a collective endeavor, a symphony of hands joined in unity. As citizens of this nation, we recognize that we are bound by an invisible thread that weaves through our hearts—a shared responsibility to leave behind a legacy of hope and sustainability.

Our journey begins with an unwavering commitment to sustainable practices. We are mindful of our environmental impact and the delicate balance between progress and preservation. Every decision we make, whether on an individual or communal level, is infused with an environmental consciousness that seeks to harmonize our progress with the earth's well-being.

We tread gently on the earth, for we understand that its splendor is not ours to exploit recklessly. Like benevolent custodians, we recognize our role as caretakers of this precious planet. Our ancestors' wisdom serves as a guiding light, reminding us of the interconnectedness of all life and the importance of nurturing the earth that sustains us.

Our commitment to cherishing the environment is evident from bustling cities to the tranquil countryside. We plant trees to rejuvenate the land, protect endangered species to ensure biodiversity and advocate for sustainable energy sources to reduce our carbon footprint. Through education and awareness, we empower every citizen to become an advocate for change, fostering a sense of environmental stewardship that transcends generations.

The journey of sustainable practices is a testament to our unwavering belief in a brighter tomorrow. We know the path ahead will be arduous, fraught with challenges and obstacles.

Yet, with each step we take, we draw strength from the collective will of our people, from the knowledge that we are not alone in this pursuit of a sustainable future.

As architects of our destiny, we embrace this transformative journey with open hearts and minds. The mistakes of the past do not bind us, nor are we confined by the limitations imposed upon us. We recognize that our collective strength lies in our diversity and the myriad of voices and ideas that unite in harmony.

In the crucible of time, our unity will forge a new identity—a phoenix rising from the ashes of the past. As citizens, we have ignited a flame of hope, illuminating the path to a future where happiness, prosperity, and peace reign. With each sustainable action we take, with each gentle step, we tread upon the earth, we leave an indelible mark on the tapestry of history.

We stand at the precipice of possibility, gazing toward the horizon of our destiny. The road ahead is long, but we walk it with courage and conviction, knowing that, as citizens, we have the power to shape a world that we can proudly pass down to future generations. Together, we sow the seeds of change, cultivating a legacy of sustainability and preserving the splendor of our environment for all who will follow in our footsteps.

12-2 Brushstrokes of Change: Citizens as Architects of Transformation

In the intricate tapestry of a nation, each citizen is a vital piece of the puzzle, a unique brushstroke on the canvas of change. As the architects of our nation's future, we wield the power to paint a portrait of progress, unity, and prosperity.

Just as an artist brings life to a canvas through deliberate brushstrokes, citizens infuse vitality into the fabric of society with their actions, choices, and collective will. Everyone's contribution, however small it may seem, creates a ripple effect, intertwining with others to form the grand tapestry of transformation.

Recognizing our free will is the ignition that sparks the flame of change within us. It is the realization that our voice matters, our actions count, and our convictions can shape the course of history. As we acknowledge this power, we shed the cloak of passivity and become the protagonists of our nation's narrative.

With free will comes responsibility—a profound responsibility to steward our nation with wisdom, empathy, and integrity. As proactive participants in its transformation, we actively engage in nation-building, working together to create an environment where each citizen can thrive and contribute.

When we unite as citizens, we become a collective force, driving progress, and shaping policies that reflect our shared values. We recognize that the strength of our nation lies in its diversity—a vibrant palette of cultures, beliefs, and perspectives. By celebrating this diversity and fostering inclusivity, we draw upon the richness of our collective experiences, enriching the tapestry of our nation with vivid hues.

Just as an artist brings harmony to a painting by skillfully blending colors, citizens foster harmony within their nation by seeking common ground, embracing compromise, and finding solutions that benefit all. We set aside divisive ideologies and embrace the greater good, for the symphony of unity harmonizes the canvas of change.

As transformation architects, we look beyond the present, envisioning the nation we wish to bequeath to future generations. We invest in education, innovation, and sustainable practices, laying the groundwork for a legacy that endures. By planting seeds of progress today, we nurture a garden of opportunities for generations to come.

Our free will also calls us to be stewards of justice and equality, advocating for the rights of every citizen and leaving no one behind. We challenge injustices, confront systemic disparities, and create pathways for all to flourish. We paint a portrait of a just and inclusive society by empowering the marginalized and ensuring equitable access to opportunities.

With our agency, we become champions of civic engagement, actively participating in democratic processes, and making our voices heard. We vote not only as an individual expression but as a collective declaration of our commitment to shaping our nation's future. We engage in dialogue, encouraging open conversations that lead to greater understanding and cooperation.

As brushstrokes of change, we can still overcome challenges or setbacks. We persevere with unwavering determination, knowing that transformation is an iterative journey and progress often comes through trial and error. Each stroke may not be perfect, but together, they form a masterpiece that tells the story of our nation's resilience and growth.

In the grand gallery of the nation, each citizen's brushstroke adds to the beauty and complexity of the collective

portrait. As architects of our destiny, we paint with passion, purpose, and love, crafting a masterpiece that stands the test of time. Through our agency, we create a nation that shines as a beacon of hope and inspiration, inspiring generations to pick up their brushes and continue the legacy of change.

CHAPTER 13

REDEFINING IDENTITY

13-1 The Power of Citizenship in Nation Rebuilding

As citizens, we are not mere spectators in the unfolding narrative of our nation; instead, we are the architects of our collective destiny. The power to effect change resides within the hearts and hands of every citizen. In rebuilding our nation, we have a unique opportunity to harness this power, transforming our identity into a potent tool of progress and renewal.

The notion of identity is not a static concept but a dynamic force that evolves with time and circumstance. As the landscape of our nation transforms, so too must our perception of who we are as citizens. We must recognize that our identity is not bound solely by our past but stretches toward the horizon of possibilities.

Nation rebuilding is about reimagining our collective identity that transcends the scars and embraces the values and aspirations that unite citizens. We shed the divisive labels that once defined us and embraced a shared identity founded on unity, inclusivity, and empathy. In doing so, we dismantle the barriers that have hindered progress and open doors to new opportunities for growth and collaboration.

Just as architects draw upon various materials and techniques to construct a building, we, too, must utilize the tools at our disposal to rebuild our nation. Among these tools, identity transformation stands out as a potent instrument. By aligning our self-perception with the vision of a thriving and harmonious society, we create a reservoir of hope and resilience that propels us forward.

As citizens, we wield the power of unity—a force that unites our diverse voices and aspirations into a harmonious chorus. When we recognize our shared humanity and prioritize the well-being of our fellow citizens, we foster an environment of trust and cooperation. We bridge the gaps that have divided us through unity, forging a solid foundation to rebuild our nation.

Rebuilding our nation also demands we confront the past with courage and honesty. Acknowledging historical injustices and traumas enables us to heal and grow as a society. In redefining our identity, we learn from past mistakes and draw strength from the resilience that has carried us through adversity.

We must remember the individual's power in the nation's rebuilding process. Each citizen is a vital piece of the puzzle—a brushstroke on the canvas of change. When we recognize our agency in shaping the destiny of our nation, we become proactive participants in its transformation. We contribute our unique perspectives, skills, and passions to the tapestry of progress.

The transformation of identity extends beyond our nation's borders to our place within the global community. As world citizens, we embrace a broader sense of responsibility that acknowledges our interconnectedness with other countries and peoples. We collaborate with the international community, learning from their experiences and sharing our own, fostering mutual growth and understanding.

Ultimately, the power to rebuild our nation lies in its citizens' collective will and action. The change begins within each individual as we commit to embodying the values we seek to instill in our society. As architects of our destiny, we recognize that the nation-rebuilding process is not a quick fix but a continuous journey that demands dedication, patience, and resilience.

As we redefine our identity, we transcend the limitations of the past, embracing the infinite possibilities of the future. We step into our roles as stewards of progress, custodians of hope, and architects of unity. With every action we take, every choice we make, and every value we uphold, we lay the foundation for a nation reborn—a nation defined by compassion, inclusivity, and a shared commitment to building a brighter tomorrow.

CHAPTER 14

A NEW IDENTITY

14-1 Redefining People's Identification

Throughout history, leaders have exercised their authority to effect significant changes within their nations, including changing the country's name or renaming geographical landmarks. Such actions often carry symbolic and historical significance, signaling a new era, a fresh beginning, or a break from the past. However, one realm that has remained relatively untouched in these transformative processes is the personal identification of the citizens themselves.

As architects of our destiny, we now stand at the threshold of a new possibility—a groundbreaking shift in how we perceive and define our identities. Imagine a world where people have the freedom and agency to embrace a unique identification that aligns more authentically with their true selves and reflects the values of unity, inclusivity, and compassion.

In the annals of history, leaders have recognized the trans-formative power of names and their influence on the collective consciousness. Changing a country's name can symbolize a renewed sense of identity, a departure from past ideologies, or a declaration of unity. Similarly, renaming places can be an act of reconciliation or an effort to honor the indigenous heritage of the land.

However, the change in people's identification represents an unprecedented and profound step toward self-discovery and self-expression. It is an acknowledgment that, as individuals, we are not fixed entities bound by the names given at birth. Instead, we are dynamic beings, constantly evolving and deserving of a character that resonates with our deepest essence.

Redefining people's identification extends far beyond a mere superficial modification. It is a declaration of autonomy—a recognition of everyone's sovereignty over their own narrative. By reclaiming the right to choose our identification, we assert that our identities are not prescribed by others but authored by ourselves.

This transformative process invites us to question the societal norms that have dictated how we see ourselves. It challenges us to transcend the limitations of tradition, culture, and societal expectations, enabling us to craft an identity that aligns with our values, passions, and aspirations.

In embracing this change, we celebrate the rich diversity of humanity. **Each person's identification becomes a unique tapestry of experiences, dreams, and strengths they wish to carry forward.** This mosaic of identities weaves together a vibrant and harmonious human family where we celebrate differences and forge unity through mutual understanding and respect.

As with any significant shift, there may be challenges and resistance to redefining people's identification. However, it is essential to remember that this change is not about erasing history or negating the past. Instead, it is an opportunity to expand our horizons, grow as individuals and as a collective, and move forward with a shared vision of unity and compassion.

The power to redefine people's identification lies not in the hands of a few but in the collective will of the people. It is a democratic process driven by inclusivity and open dialogue. By engaging in meaningful conversations and acknowledging the diverse perspectives within society, we pave the way for a genuine transformation that empowers us all.

In conclusion, redefining people's identification is revolutionary in the quest for self-discovery and unity. As architects of our destiny, we honor our individuality, celebrate our uniqueness, and embrace the power of choice in defining who we are. In this bold self-reclamation, we sow the seeds of a more compassionate and inclusive world—where each person's identity is an authentic reflection of their true self.

14-2 Redefining Identity to Eradicate Division Among Citizens

In pursuing a harmonious and thriving society, we stand at the precipice of a profound realization—that the key to eradicating division among citizens lies in the redefinition of our collective identity. Just as scientists tirelessly search for a vaccine to combat diseases, we, as architects of our destiny, have the power to discover a potent vaccine through unity and understanding that can heal the divisions that plague our world.

In the current landscape, divisions among citizens are prevalent, whether they stem from political ideologies, cultural differences, or socioeconomic disparities. These divisions have led to fractures within communities and nations, hindering progress and sowing seeds of discord. However, by redefining our identity, we can address the root cause of this division and pave the way for a transformative shift toward unity.

Redefining our identity is not about erasing our differences or imposing a monolithic identity upon everyone. Instead, it is an invitation to recognize the humanity that unites us all—the shared aspirations, hopes, and dreams that transcend our individuality. It is an acknowledgment that, at our core, we are interconnected beings, and our well-being is intricately linked to the well-being of others.

The vaccine for unity begins with a process of self-reflection and introspection. We must examine the biases, prejudices, and preconceptions that have shaped our perceptions of others. By acknowledging our ignorance, we open ourselves to the possibility of growth and transformation.

At the heart of redefining our identity is the practice of empathy and active listening. We must seek to understand the experiences and perspectives of our fellow citizens, stepping into their shoes and seeing the world through their eyes. Through empathy, we break down the walls of division and cultivate a genuine connection and understanding.

Redefining our identity is also an act of collective healing. It involves acknowledging the wounds of the past, confronting historical injustices, and working together to forge a path of reconciliation. By recognizing the pain and trauma that specific segments of our society have endured, we create an environment of empathy and compassion, fostering a sense of belonging for all citizens.

We discover the power of dialogue and respectful discourse in redefining our identity. Instead of engaging in divisive debates that fuel hate, we come together with an open heart and mind to engage in constructive conversations. We learn to find common ground, focusing on shared values and goals rather than dwelling on our differences.

As the vaccine for unity takes effect, we witness the emergence of collective action. Citizens from all walks of life come together to work towards a shared vision, transcending race, religion, and nationality barriers. United in purpose, we become a formidable force for positive change, capable of shaping a society built on compassion and cooperation.

This vaccine is not a one-time cure but an ongoing commitment to fostering a culture of inclusivity and acceptance. As architects of our destiny, we must actively cultivate a society that celebrates diversity and recognizes the strength that lies in our unity. We reject the notion of "us" versus "them" and embrace the understanding that we are all members of the same human family.

In conclusion, the vaccine to eradicate the division among citizens lies within our grasp. By redefining our identity, we tap into the power of empathy, dialogue, and collective action to heal the wounds of division and create a more united and harmonious society. As we embrace our shared humanity and recognize the interconnectedness that binds us, we pave the way for a future built on unity, understanding, and mutual respect. The journey towards a world free of division begins with each of us as we bravely redefine our identity and be the catalysts of positive change.

CHAPTER 15

THE EVER-EVOLVING IDENTITY

15-1 Redefining Ourselves as Architects of Destiny
In the book of Genesis, the Divine Creator demonstrates a profound act of redefining identity through the universe's creation process. As architects of our destiny, we, too, are called to embrace the ever-evolving nature of our identity, adapting and redefining ourselves according to the changing tides of time. Just as God's creation unfolded in layers of complexity, our identity is a tapestry woven from the threads of experiences, values, and aspirations that shape our journey.

The creation story in Genesis teaches us that God's design of identity is dynamic and purposeful. The Divine Architect meticulously crafted each aspect of creation, setting the stage for an unfolding narrative of growth and transformation. Similarly, as architects of our destiny, we must recognize that our identity is not unchangeable but a fluid and evolving expression of our essence.

Just as God separated the light from darkness and created order out of chaos, we, too, are called to discern the different facets of our identity. As life presents diverse experiences and challenges, we discover new dimensions of ourselves, shedding old beliefs and embracing new perspectives. Our identity is a mosaic of various traits, thoughts, and emotions that shape who we are at any given moment.

As architects of our destiny, we must be open to self-discovery and self-rediscovery. Just as God's creation unfolded step by step, our understanding of self deepens with time and experience. We learn from the tapestry of our past, draw strength from our present, and envision the possibilities of our future.

Our identity is crucial in defining our path in the grand symphony of existence. Just as God created each being with a unique purpose, our identity informs our passions, dreams, and aspirations. We embrace our authenticity, letting go of societal expectations and embracing the truth of who we must be in rebuilding our nation.

Moreover, our identity is not static but responsive to the call of the times. As architects of our destiny, we must respond to the present moment's needs. We adapt our identity to respond to the challenges and opportunities that arise, just as God responded to the changing landscape of creation.

Redefining our identity also involves shedding limiting beliefs and self-imposed constraints. Just as God's creation was boundless in its diversity, our identity has limitless potential. We free ourselves from the chains of self-doubt, embracing the expansiveness of our being and allowing ourselves to explore new horizons of growth and self-expression.

Just as God breathed life into creation, we, too, can breathe life into our identity through our intentions and actions. We infuse our identity with purpose, imbuing it with the energy of passion and dedication. With each step we take, we create a ripple effect, influencing not only our lives but also the lives of those around us.

In redefining our identity, we must also remember the importance of self-compassion. Just as God looked upon creation with love and saw that it was good, we must embrace ourselves with kindness and acceptance. We acknowledge that growth is a journey, and our identity is a work in progress—a masterpiece.

Redefining our identity as architects of our destiny is not linear but cyclical. Like the changing seasons in nature, our identity goes through cycles of growth, shedding, and renewal. With each cycle, we refine and redefine ourselves, continuously evolving into the best version of who we can be.

As architects of our destiny, we embrace the call to redefine our identity in harmony with the rhythm of time.

We honor the dynamic nature of our being, remaining open to the unfolding possibilities that lie ahead. Through this journey of self-discovery and self-rediscovery, we unveil the masterpiece of our identity—a testament to our unique place in the grand symphony of existence.

15- 2 The Family as the Catalyst for Societal Transformation: Embracing Unity Beyond Tribal Affiliations

The transformation of a society is a multifaceted process that finds its roots within the family—a microcosm of the broader community in which individuals are identified with different **"social codes," such as Sangwabutaka, Hutu, Tutsi, or Ganwa within a family, based on their birth month.** However, as we embark on a journey of healing and progress, the family becomes the catalyst for embracing unity beyond these tribal affiliations, nurturing a society built on empathy, understanding, and mutual respect.

Breaking Down Historical Barriers: The diverse identities within a family, historically separated by "fake tribes," provide an opportunity to break down the barriers that once divided them. As family members come together, they share everyday experiences, joys, and sorrows. This shared bond fosters a kinship that transcends artificial labels and historical divisions.

Families can confront historical wounds by engaging in open and honest conversations about the past, working towards forgiveness and reconciliation. This process empowers them to build bridges of understanding, dismantling the prejudices that once defined their relationships.

Fostering Empathy and Compassion: As family members from different "fake tribes" come together, they gain unique insights into each other's experiences and perspectives. This experiential exchange nurtures empathy and compassion as individuals begin to see the world through each other's eyes.

Empathy drives societal transformation as family members learn to acknowledge and understand each other's pain and struggles. This newfound compassion extends beyond the family unit, guiding them toward embracing other community members with similar openness and understanding.

Cultivating a Shared Identity: As the family transcends the limitations of "fake tribes," they develop a collective consciousness that binds them together.

Family members build a strong foundation for societal transformation by focusing on their shared values and aspirations. This shared identity serves as a reminder that unity is not defined by tribal affiliations but by a commitment to building a just and equitable society.

Leading by Example: The transformation within the family becomes a model for the broader community. As they embrace unity beyond "fake tribes," they become agents of change, inspiring others to follow suit. By leading by example, the family demonstrates that societal transformation begins with the collective efforts of individuals.

Their actions speak volumes, showing the community that embracing unity and breaking down tribal barriers is possible and essential for building a thriving society. This ripple effect extends beyond the family, as neighbors, friends, and acquaintances are

encouraged to challenge their preconceived notions and prejudices.

Celebrating Diversity: As the family transcends the confines
of tribal affiliations, they celebrate their diversity as a source of
strength. Each member brings unique perspectives, skills, and
experiences that enrich the family's collective journey.

This celebration of diversity becomes a powerful narrative
for societal transformation. It promotes the understanding that
unity does not entail erasing individual identities but cherishing
and weaving them into a vibrant tapestry of coexistence.

Nurturing Future Generations: The family's transformation shapes future generations' outlook. Children raised in an
environment of unity and empathy grow up with an inherent
commitment to a society free from historical divisions.

**As they carry the lessons learned from their families into
the world, they become ambassadors for societal transformation.** The cycle of healing and progress continues as they pass on
the values of unity, respect, and inclusivity to their own families
and communities.

In conclusion, the transformation of our society begins within
the family—a dynamic space where individuals identified with
different "social codes" can come together and embrace unity
beyond these historical divisions. As architects of our destiny, we
recognize that the family plays a pivotal role in building a society
founded on empathy, understanding, and mutual respect.

**By breaking down barriers, fostering empathy, and cele-
brating diversity, the family becomes a powerful catalyst for
societal transformation.** The lessons learned within the family
unit extend beyond its boundaries, guiding us toward a brighter

future where unity prevails, and a collective commitment to progress replaces historical divisions.

15-3 Nurturing the Garden of Love as a Family

In the fertile landscape of a family, planting is not merely sowing seeds in the soil but also sowing the seeds of compassion, kindness, and empathy in the hearts of its members. Like tender saplings, these seeds may appear small and inconspicuous initially, but their potential to flourish and blossom is boundless. As architects of love and understanding, the family plays a pivotal role in nurturing these seeds, watering them with acts of love, compassion, and acceptance.

To plant the seed of compassion is to cultivate a deep sense of empathy within the family. It is the ability to step into each other's shoes, feel the joys and sorrows, and offer a supportive embrace. Compassion strengthens the family bond, fostering an environment where each member feels seen, heard, and valued.

Kindness, like a gentle breeze, sweeps through the family garden, nourishing the seedlings of connection and affection. It is the practice of small gestures of thoughtfulness, consideration, and generosity that breathe life into relationships. Kindness becomes the balm that heals wounds and brings solace to weary hearts in moments of vulnerability and conflict.

Empathy is the family's guiding compass, directing each member toward more profound understanding and emotional attunement. It fosters open communication and active listening, creating a safe space for sharing thoughts, feelings, and aspirations. Empathy is the key that unlocks doors of mutual respect and reinforces the unity of the family.

Just as gardens require diligent care, a family's seeds of compassion, kindness, and empathy demand constant nurturing. Time and attention must be devoted to tending to these tender sprouts. Family members must be attuned to one another's needs and emotions, offering reassurance, support, and validation.

Watering these seeds involves acts of love that cascade through the family like a gentle rain. It is in the affectionate hugs shared at the start of the day, the words of encouragement whispered during difficult times, and the laughter that echoes through the walls, uniting hearts in joy.

Understanding serves as the nutrient-rich soil, sustaining the growing garden of love. It involves setting aside judgment and embracing acceptance, acknowledging that each member is unique and imperfect yet worthy of love and belonging. Understanding nurtures the seedlings of trust and lays the foundation for a strong and resilient family bond.

Acceptance is the sunshine that warms the family garden, allowing each member to bloom and grow authentically. It affirms that the family remains a sanctuary of love and support regardless of differences and challenges. Acceptance celebrates the individuality of each member and cultivates an atmosphere of unconditional love.

Growth takes time and patience in the nurturing embrace of a family garden. Just as flowers do not bloom overnight, the seeds of compassion, kindness, and empathy may take time to flourish fully. Family members must practice patience, knowing that growth is a journey and transformation happens with dedication and commitment.

As the family garden blooms with compassion, kindness, and empathy, it becomes a sanctuary of love, a place of refuge and rejuvenation for each member. It becomes a haven where hearts find solace and souls find respite from the challenges of the outside world.

In planting the seeds of compassion, kindness, and empathy as a family, a harmonious symphony of love unfolds. Each member becomes a gardener, nurturing the shared values and principles that bind them together. The family garden becomes a testament to the beauty of unconditional love, and its blossoms radiate a light that brightens the world beyond its borders.

In nurturing this family garden, may we embrace the transformative power of compassion, kindness, and empathy. Let us sow the seeds of love and understanding and watch our family flourish in a tapestry of unity and joy. Together, we create a legacy—a garden of love that will continue to bloom and inspire future generations.

15-4 Sowing the Seeds Across Generations

In the timeless tapestry of family, the seeds of compassion, kindness, and empathy possess a unique and remarkable quality —they have the potential to transcend generations. Just as a mighty oak tree begins as a tiny acorn, these seeds can take root and grow when nurtured with care and intention, leaving an indelible mark on the family's legacy.

Like a living organism, the family evolves and adapts with each generation. Within this ever-changing landscape, the seeds of compassion, kindness, and empathy find their fertile ground. As one generation sows these seeds, the subsequent ones reap the harvest, carrying forward the virtues and values that form the foundation of the family's strength.

The transmission of compassion from one generation to the next is an inheritance of profound significance. When children witness acts of compassion and empathy from their parents and elders, they learn the value of caring for others and the art of kindness towards themselves. They observe the power of a helping hand, a listening ear, and a compassionate heart, and in turn, they grow to become beacons of light, illuminating the lives of others.

Kindness, too, becomes a thread that weaves through the fabric of generations. It manifests in the smallest gestures—a smile, a word of encouragement, a random act of generosity. As family members practice kindness towards one another, they create a ripple effect that extends far beyond the immediate circle. The legacy of kindness inspires future generations, encouraging them to carry forward this legacy of warmth and benevolence.

Empathy, the cornerstone of meaningful connections, is a gift passed from generation to generation. When family members listen with open hearts, validate each other's emotions, and seek to understand one another's perspectives, they forge bonds that transcend time. Empathy fosters trust, where each generation feels valued and accepted, encouraging them to embrace their uniqueness while cultivating compassion for others.

As the seeds of compassion, kindness, and empathy take root in the hearts of family members, they create a virtuous cycle of love and understanding. The children, witnessing these qualities in their elders, are inspired to embody these virtues, perpetuating the cycle for generations to come. Like a never-ending relay race, the baton of compassion, kindness, and empathy is passed from hand to hand, ensuring that the light of these virtues continues to shine brightly.

However, this transgenerational transmission of virtues requires patience and commitment. Just as a tree takes years to reach its full stature, the growth of compassion, kindness, and empathy is a journey that spans lifetimes. Family members must practice patience, knowing that transformation takes time and dedication. They understand that each generation contributes its part to the ongoing saga of the family's evolution.

With dedication and commitment, family members tend to the garden of virtues, tending to the seeds with love and care. They understand that the growth of compassion, kindness, and empathy is not a solitary pursuit but a collective endeavor. Each generation plays a vital role in sowing, nurturing, and reaping the fruits of these seeds, ensuring that the legacy of love and understanding endures.

In sowing the seeds of compassion, kindness, and empathy across generations, the family becomes a sanctuary of love—a place where hearts find solace, acceptance knows no bounds, and the flame of empathy continues to burn brightly. As the torchbearers of these timeless virtues, the family illuminates the world beyond its borders, leaving a lasting impact on the lives of countless others.

Together, hand in hand, heart to heart, the family weaves a story of compassion, kindness, and empathy—a tale that spans generations and shapes the course of history. In this beautiful symphony of love, the family discovers its true legacy, etched not in material possessions but in the immeasurable wealth of virtues passed down from generation to generation.

CHAPTER 16

TRANSFORMING SOCIETY THROUGH INCLUSIVE SYMBOLS

16-1 Identity Cards for Mind Vaccination

In the pursuit of transforming our society towards empathy, understanding, and mutual respect, the distribution of new identity cards matching the month of birth to the "social code" serves as a symbolic step towards vaccinating our minds against divisive notions and fostering a more inclusive society. These identity cards are powerful tools to challenge historical divisions and promote a collective identity that celebrates our humanity. By embracing this transformative approach, we set in motion a journey of healing and progress, paving the way for a society united by empathy and compassion.

A Symbolic Gesture of Unity: The distribution of new identity cards based on the month of birth symbolizes a unifying gesture. This approach challenges the divisive labels that once defined us by emphasizing our physical appearance whereas we are citizens of the same nation.

The new identity cards become a tangible representation of our commitment to unity and inclusivity. They are a visual reminder that we are no more tribal affiliations but a collective whole with shared aspirations for a harmonious society.

Fostering an Inclusive Identity: The new identity cards promote an inclusive national identity. As citizens receive new identity cards, they are encouraged to embrace the diversity within their communities and recognize that their individuality is not confined to historical divisions. This approach nurtures a sense of belonging and pride in being part of a society that values inclusivity and celebrates diversity. The new identity cards become symbols of a progressive culture where unity prevails over division.

Mind Vaccination: The act of distributing new identity cards based on birth month is akin to vaccinating our minds against the spread of divisive ideologies. It challenges prejudiced mindsets and encourages citizens to break free from the shackles of historical animosities.

Through this process, our minds are immunized against negative perceptions, enabling us to view each other through a lens of empathy and understanding. The mind vaccination paves the way for fruitful dialogues and interactions, fostering a society where cooperation and mutual respect thrive.

Transforming Societal Perception: The distribution of new identity cards prompts a shift in societal perception. It signals a departure from the past's divisive practices and a stride towards embracing unity and harmony.

As these new identity cards become commonplace, the once prominent "fake tribes" are relegated to history, and a new narrative of a united society emerges. This transformation in societal perception has a cascading effect on policies, interactions, and attitudes within the nation.

Encouraging Dialogue and Reconciliation: Distributing new identity cards presents open dialogue and reconciliation opportunities. It enables citizens to converse about historical divisions, acknowledge past grievances, and work together toward healing.

As individuals come together to discuss their shared history, they gain a deeper understanding of each other's experiences, fostering empathy and compassion. These conversations become stepping stones towards reconciliation, guiding the nation towards a brighter and more harmonious future.

Strengthening the Collective Journey: The distribution of new identity cards becomes a pivotal moment in the collective transformation journey. It signifies a turning point, where citizens collectively commit to building a society free from the constraints of divisive labels.

With each new identity card distributed, the momentum of societal transformation grows stronger. Citizens unite in their quest for a more inclusive and compassionate society, demonstrating that positive change is not a distant dream but an achievable reality.

In conclusion, the distribution of new identity cards matching birth month represents a transformative step

towards vaccinating our minds and reshaping our society. Through this symbolic gesture of unity and inclusivity, we challenge divisive notions and pave the way for a harmonious nation. The new identity cards become potent symbols of our collective journey of healing and progress, guiding us toward a society where empathy and compassion reign supreme. As architects of our destiny, we recognize that this transformation begins with a single step—the distribution of identity cards that promise a brighter and more united future.

16-1 a. Identity Cards Reflecting Commonality Over Divisive Labels are a Unifying Gesture

The distribution of new identity cards matching the "social codes" to the "month of birth" rather than physical attributes such as the shape of the face, nose, or height serves as a powerful and symbolic gesture of unity. This approach challenges the divisive labels that once defined us by emphasizing our physical appearance whereas we are citizens of the same nation. Through this unifying gesture, we embark on a transformative journey that celebrates our collective humanity and redefines our national identity based on inclusivity, empathy, and understanding.

Shifting the Paradigm: The distribution of identity cards based on birth month represents a paradigm shift from historical practices focusing on physical attributes to categorizing individuals into "fake tribes." Moving away from such divisive labeling, we acknowledge the limitations of these criteria in defining our shared identity as a nation.

This new approach challenges deep-rooted prejudices and biases, encouraging citizens to see beyond physical differences and recognize the richness of diversity within the nation.

Emphasizing Commonality: The identity cards, based on the birth month, emphasize the commonality that binds all citizens together. Regardless of their background or physical attributes, everyone shares the experience of being born in the same month and contributing to their collective identity.

This emphasis on commonality fosters a sense of unity and belonging, promoting a national consciousness that transcends divisive labels and focuses on our shared values and aspirations.

Fostering Inclusivity: The distribution of identity cards based on birth month promotes a culture of inclusivity. It sends a powerful message that every citizen is an integral part of the nation, regardless of their heritage or physical appearance.

By acknowledging the diverse backgrounds within the nation, we create a society that is open, accepting, and welcoming to all, valuing the unique contributions of everyone.

Nurturing Empathy and Understanding: This unifying gesture encourages citizens to cultivate empathy and understanding towards one another. By recognizing the shared experience of being identified by the same month of birth, individuals begin to relate to each other on a human level beyond the boundaries of "fake tribes."

This newfound empathy forms the basis for meaningful connections and fosters a culture of compassion and support within the society.

Building Bridges of Connection: The distribution of identity cards based on birth month creates bridges of connection between individuals from different backgrounds. As citizens interact and engage with others holding similar identity cards, they discover shared interests and experiences that unite them.

These bridges of connection promote social cohesion and build a sense of community that extends beyond tribal affiliations, fostering cooperation and collaboration.

A Foundation for Social Progress: By embracing this unifying gesture, we lay the foundation for social progress and transformation. The shift from divisive labeling to a focus on commonality opens opportunities for constructive dialogue, reconciliation, and collective action.

This new perspective fuels initiatives to address historical grievances, promote social justice, and build a more equitable society for all citizens.

In conclusion, the distribution of identity cards matching the "social code" to the month of birth symbolizes a unifying gesture that challenges divisive labels and fosters a sense of commonality among citizens. This approach promotes inclusivity, empathy, and understanding by emphasizing our shared identity as members of the same nation.

Through this transformative journey, we redefine our national identity as one that celebrates diversity and values every individual's unique contribution. As architects of our destiny, we recognize that this symbolic gesture is not just about identity cards but represents a profound shift in our collective consciousness—a step towards a harmonious and united society that thrives on the power of empathy and shared humanity.

16-1 b. Identity Cards Based on Shared Experiences Represent a Tapestry of Commonality

The distribution of identity cards based on the month of birth weaves a tapestry of commonality that binds all citizens together. This approach emphasizes the shared experience of being born in the same season of the year and in the same nation. This approach transcends the confines of physical attributes and historical divisions, fostering a collective identity rooted in unity and shared humanity.

Celebrating Shared Experiences: The identity cards, linked to the month of birth, celebrate the shared experiences that unite all citizens. Everyone shares the profound journey of entering the world during a specific year's season, regardless of their background or physical appearance.

This celebration of shared experiences cultivates a sense of belonging and interconnectedness, promoting the understanding that we are all part of the intricate fabric of the nation's history and progress.

A Unified National Identity: By emphasizing the commonality of being born in the same nation, the identity cards contribute to a unified national identity. This collective consciousness recognizes that despite our diverse backgrounds and histories, we are all integral to the nation's story.

This unified national identity fosters a sense of citizen pride and ownership, instilling a shared responsibility for the nation's well-being and progress.

Breaking Down Historical Divisions: The identity cards based on birth month serve as a potent tool for breaking down historical divisions rooted in physical attributes or tribal affiliations. The cards challenge deep-seated prejudices and biases by focusing on shared experiences rather than divisive labels.

This transformative approach opens the door to healing historical wounds, fostering understanding, and promoting reconciliation between different communities within the nation.

Nurturing a Culture of Inclusivity: The identity cards underscore the importance of inclusivity in our collective identity. Regardless of their background, every citizen becomes an equal participant in the nation's journey, contributing to its growth and development.

This culture of inclusivity extends beyond the distribution of identity cards, permeating various aspects of societal life, from education and employment to governance and decision-making.

Encouraging Collective Responsibility: The emphasis on shared experiences through identity cards fosters a sense of collective responsibility for the nation's well-being. Citizens recognize that they are interconnected and interdependent, each contributing to the nation's tapestry of progress.

This collective responsibility empowers citizens to shape the nation's future actively, working together towards a harmonious and prosperous society.

Bridging Communities and Generations: The identity cards become bridges that connect different communities and generations. As citizens encounter others who share the same birth month, they discover connections beyond physical attributes or tribal affiliations.

These bridges of commonality promote intergenerational understanding and cohesion, nurturing a sense of continuity and unity that spans time.

In conclusion, the distribution of identity cards based on the birth month emphasizes the commonality that binds all citizens together. By celebrating shared experiences and fostering a unified national identity, this transformative approach breaks down historical divisions and nurtures a culture of inclusivity and collective responsibility.

As architects of our destiny, we recognize the power of this symbolic gesture in weaving a tapestry of commonality that transcends physical attributes and tribal affiliations. Embracing our shared humanity, we step into a future where empathy, unity, and understanding form the fabric of our harmonious society.

16-2 A Flag of Unity: The Impact of a Transformed National Flag in Our Minds and Daily Lives

A national flag is a powerful symbol that embodies the essence of a nation's identity. It waves proudly, representing its people's collective values, history, and aspirations. However, as we embark on a journey of identity transformation, the need for a flag that reflects our newfound unity and shared humanity becomes evident. A national flag that embraces our diverse heritage while promoting empathy and inclusivity can profoundly impact our minds and daily lives, constantly reminding us of our collective journey toward a harmonious society.

Embracing Diversity: The transformed national flag should celebrate the diversity within the nation while emphasizing our unity as a single entity. The flag becomes a tapestry of inclusivity by incorporating elements representing different cultures, traditions, and histories.

Each citizen sees their heritage reflected in the flag, fostering a sense of pride and belonging to a nation that values and celebrates its rich diversity.

Symbolizing Unity: While embracing diversity, the transformed national flag should symbolize unity. It can achieve this through colors or patterns that blend seamlessly together, demonstrating the harmony of different elements coming together as one.

The flag becomes a visual representation of our collective strength, reminding us that we are stronger together, united by shared values and aspirations.

Fostering a Sense of Identity: The transformed national flag instills citizens' sense of identity and belonging. As they see the flag waving proudly in various settings, it becomes a symbol that unites people from different backgrounds under a shared vision.

This sense of identity strengthens the national fabric, cultivating a shared responsibility for the nation's growth and prosperity.

Encouraging Pride and Respect: A national flag reflecting identity transformation encourages citizens to take pride in their nation's progress toward unity and empathy. As they witness the flag waving in public spaces, at events, and during national celebrations, it evokes respect and admiration for their collective journey.

The flag becomes a source of inspiration, reminding citizens of the transformative power they possess in shaping their society.

Impacting Daily Lives: The presence of the transformed national flag in our daily lives has a far-reaching impact. It creates an atmosphere of unity and belonging, fostering community beyond tribal affiliations or differences.

The flag's symbolism influences interactions, conversations, and decision-making processes, promoting empathy and understanding in daily exchanges.

A Beacon of Hope: The transformed national flag is a beacon of hope for future generations. Children growing up under this flag are exposed to a visual representation of unity and inclusivity, inspiring them to carry forward the values of empathy and acceptance.

The flag becomes a legacy that transcends generations, guiding the nation toward an even brighter and more harmonious future.

In conclusion, a national flag reflecting the identity transformation is a powerful tool for changing our minds and impacting our daily lives. By embracing diversity while symbolizing unity, the flag becomes a source of pride, respect, and inspiration for citizens. Its presence fosters a sense of identity and belonging, influencing daily interactions, and shaping the nation's collective consciousness.

As architects of our destiny, we recognize the significance of a transformed national flag in guiding our society toward empathy, unity, and mutual respect. Embracing this symbolic representation, we march forward with renewed hope and determination, unfurling a flag that reflects the strength of our shared humanity and the power of our collective transformation.

16-3 A New Currency: Symbolizing Healing and Unity

In the transformative journey of Burundi SAHUTUGA, every aspect of the nation's identity is carefully crafted to reflect unity, inclusivity, and healing. As part of this holistic approach, the government introduces a new currency, the **BSF (Burundi Sahutuga Franc)**, which carries profound symbolism and represents more than just economic transactions.

Currency as a Symbol of Renewal: In Burundi SAHUTUGA, the currency is more than just a medium of exchange; it symbolizes the nation's rebirth and a testament to the shared commitment to healing and unity. The new currency, **BSF**, embodies the nation's core values and aspirations.

Deciphering the Currency Code: The currency code **BS** holds a dual significance. **'B'** stands for 'Burundi,' representing the geographical and cultural roots of the nation. **'S,'** on the other hand, signifies 'Sahutuga,' the unifying name adopted to redefine the collective identity beyond historical divisions.

Healing Through Symbols: Symbols have the power to transcend words and evoke profound emotions. In the case of the **BSF** currency, every transaction becomes a reminder of the nation's transformation—a reminder that unity and inclusivity drive the nation's progress.

The Currency's Design: The design of the **BSF** currency is a work of art. It features imagery that celebrates the nation's diversity and natural beauty. Icons representing various groups coexist harmoniously, showcasing that in Burundi SAHUTUGA, unity is strength.

A Tool for Economic Prosperity: While laden with symbolism, the **BSF** currency also serves a practical purpose in fostering economic prosperity. It facilitates trade, investment, and financial stability, laying the economic foundation for the nation's growth.

A Beacon of Hope: The introduction of the **BSF** currency is a beacon of hope for Burundi SAHUTUGA. It symbolizes a fresh start, a break from past divisions, and a commitment to building a brighter future together.

Conclusion

In Burundi SAHUTUGA, the **BSF** currency is more than just money; it's a tangible representation of the nation's transformation. It carries with it the aspirations of a united people who have chosen to rewrite their history, heal old wounds, and forge a new destiny together. The **BSF** currency is a reminder that symbols imbued with meaning, can inspire profound change, and serve as a testament to the resilience of a nation on its path to becoming a true paradise in Africa.

16-4 Monuments of Healing: Embracing Forgiveness and Reconciliation

In the tapestry of our nation's history, the threads of conflict and suffering are interwoven, etching scars upon our collective memory. Yet, as architects of our destiny, we stand at the crossroads of a transformative choice to observe our past, heal our wounds, and forge a future defined by forgiveness and reconciliation. This chapter explores the profound significance of remembrance and unity as we embark on a journey to build monuments of healing and mark a month that holds the key to redemption.

A Tribute to Lives Lost. Our hearts bear the weight of shared loss, the echoes of lives extinguished by the turmoil of civil strife. Each soul departed left behind a legacy of pain and remembrance, and our solemn duty is to honor their memory. The decision to build monuments to remember our beloved ones, adorned with the timeless inscription **"No more bloodshed,"** is a testament to our commitment to peace and unity.

October: A Month of Reflection. In the annals of October lie poignant markers of our traumatic history. In October, we bid farewell to the valiant hero of our independence. We mourned the loss of the first democratically elected president and our countless innocent family members killed after his assassination. October is a month of collective reflection and remembrance —a reminder that even amidst our differences, we can come together to mourn, heal, and embrace the path of reconciliation.

Unity in Mourning. The monuments we erect are not merely stone and mortar; they embody our commitment to unity. In every town, the mark **"No more bloodshed"** etched in stone speaks a universal language that transcends divisions and resonates with the desire for a harmonious future. As we gather around these monuments, we stand united in our sorrow, our determination to prevent further bloodshed, and our pursuit of reconciliation.

Redeeming the Time Through Commemoration. Commemorating together is a powerful act of redemption—a reclamation of the time lost to conflict and a pledge to pave a new path forward. By pausing to remember the lives sacrificed to the fires of strife, we kindle the flame of understanding, compassion, and empathy. We forge a bond that surpasses the boundaries of political affiliations and sow the seeds of healing that will flourish for generations to come.

A Month of Reconciliation. October becomes more than a month of reflection; it becomes a month of reconciliation—a period when we extend our hands to one another, listen to each other's stories, and embrace the ideals of forgiveness and unity. Through shared moments of commemoration, we foster an environment where wounds can mend, divisions can dissolve, and the promise of a harmonious future can replace the scars of the past.

Architects of Healing. As we raise these monuments, we become architects of healing, sculptors of a destiny marked by unity and reconciliation. The inscription **"No more bloodshed"** is not just a declaration; it is a vow—a vow to honor the lives lost, to protect the lives that remain, and to build a society where conflict is replaced by dialogue, where wounds are replaced by understanding, and where the pain is transformed into a legacy of unity.

A Call to Unite. Inscribed upon these monuments are not only words but a call to action to unite as one transformed nation. In our collective remembrance, we find strength. In our shared grief, we find solace. And in our commitment to forgiveness and reconciliation, we find the keys to unlocking a future untainted by the horrors of the past. Let us stand together, hand in hand, as we build these monuments of healing, for they stand as symbols of our resolve to forge a path of unity, peace, and enduring harmony.

16-5 Streets of Honor: Commemorating Unity and Democracy

As the sun rises over the landscapes of our transformed nation, it illuminates not only the physical roads that stretch across our land but also the paths forged by the heroes who fought for unity, democracy, and national integrity. These heroes, whose unwavering dedication has shaped our collective destiny, deserve to be honored in ways that echo through the corridors of time. Through the dedication of streets bearing their names, we immortalize their legacy and ensure their stories continue to inspire us.

Guardians of Unity: A Legacy Honored

From the bustling cities to the tranquil towns, our transformed nation's streets are imbued with the legacy of those who championed unity. These heroes understood that a united populace is the bedrock upon which a prosperous nation stands. Through their sacrifices, they bridged divides and sowed the seeds of camaraderie, inspiring us to embrace the strength of our diversity and forge a cohesive society.

Champions of Democracy: Echoes of Freedom

The essence of our transformed nation rests upon the ideals of democracy—where every voice is heard, every vote counts, and every citizen plays a role in shaping the destiny of our land. The heroes who fought for these principles have etched their names into the annals of history. By gracing our streets with their names, we pay homage to their tireless efforts and ensure that the torch of democracy continues to burn brightly.

Sentinels of National Integrity: A Commitment Honored

National integrity is the cornerstone of a thriving nation. The heroes who safeguarded our nation's integrity did so with unwavering devotion. As their names grace the streets that wind through our towns and cities, we declare our commitment to upholding the values they defended—the values that bind us together as citizens of a transformed nation, Burundi SAHUTUGA.

Inspiration in Every Corner: Living Memorials

Every street with the name of a unity, democracy, or integrity champion becomes a living memorial—a place where their spirit continues to inspire us. As we walk these streets, we are reminded of the sacrifices, battles, and victories achieved in pursuing a united, democratic, and morally sound society.

A Future Shaped by the Past: Lessons Learned

The dedication of streets to our heroes is not just a gesture of gratitude; it's a reminder that our present and future are deeply rooted in the actions of those who came before us. Their stories serve as beacons of light, guiding us through challenges and illuminating the path toward progress.

Unity in Diversity: Heroes for All

From rural roads to urban avenues, the names of our heroes are proudly displayed, transcending regions, backgrounds, and walks of life. This inclusivity is a testament to the fact that unity, democracy, and integrity know no boundaries.

A Call to Remembrance: Preserving the Past for the Future

In dedicating streets to our heroes, we preserve their memory for generations. These streets are not just thoroughfares; they are monuments of remembrance that remind us of the virtues we hold dear.

Our Shared Responsibility: Building on Their Legacy

As citizens of a transformed nation, we are entrusted with upholding the ideals championed by these heroes. By walking the streets that bear their names, we pledge to continue their legacy—working tirelessly to cultivate unity, uphold democracy, and safeguard our national integrity.

Conclusion: A Journey of Honor

As we traverse the streets of our transformed nation, may the names etched upon them serve as a constant reminder of the indomitable spirit that drives us forward. With unity in our hearts, democracy in our principles, and integrity in our actions, we embark on a journey that honors the heroes of our past while shaping a future that stands as a testament to their courage and dedication.

CHAPTER 17

THE TRANSFORMED FAMILY TREE

17-1 Cultivating Genuine Connection and Understanding

In the branches of a family tree lies a profound potential to transcend the walls of division that have divided societies for generations. As architects of our destiny, we can transform our family tree, breaking free from the shackles of prejudice and hate and cultivating a space of genuine connection and understanding.

The family tree is a testament to our shared ancestry—a living record of our forebears' stories, struggles, and triumphs. In these roots, we find the foundation of our beliefs, traditions, and values. However, just as trees grow crooked from unfavorable conditions, our family tree may bear the burden of historical biases and deep-rooted divisions passed down through generations.

Through introspection and self-awareness, we begin the process of transformation. We examine the branches of our family tree, confronting the biases and prejudices that may have influenced our upbringing. As we peel back the layers of history, we gain insight into the cultural and societal influences that have shaped our identity.

Transforming the family tree requires courageous conversations—a willingness to explore the stories that have been left untold, the experiences that have been silenced, and the perspectives that have been marginalized. By creating a space of openness and vulnerability, we allow each family member to share their unique narrative, fostering an environment of trust and understanding.

The process of transformation has its challenges. Just as pruning a tree requires cutting away deadwood to promote growth, we must confront uncomfortable truths and relinquish outdated beliefs that no longer serve us. It may require unearthing painful memories or addressing family rifts, but through this process, we pave the way for healing and growth.

As the family tree transforms, a new sense of connection emerges—one rooted in empathy and compassion. We recognize that our shared history binds us, and we embrace the diversity of experiences that make each branch unique. Through this understanding, we shed the labels of "us" versus "them," and we begin to see each other as fellow travelers on life's journey.

In cultivating genuine connection and understanding, we celebrate the richness of our family's heritage. We embrace the traditions that bring us joy, the customs that connect us to our roots, and the values that guide our moral compass. At the same time, we also learn to appreciate and respect the diversity of perspectives and choices within the family, recognizing that everyone's path is uniquely theirs.

As the transformation extends to future generations, the family tree becomes a powerful force for positive change. The values of empathy, understanding, and inclusivity are passed down as an enduring legacy—a legacy that transcends familial boundaries and ripples out into the world.

Beyond the confines of the family, the transformed family tree becomes a symbol of hope and possibility—a testament to the power of love to bridge divides and heal wounds. It inspires others to embark on their transformation journey, creating a collective movement towards a more compassionate and understanding society.

In conclusion, through the transformation of our family tree, we hold the key to breaking down the walls of division and cultivating a space of genuine connection and understanding. The journey begins with self-awareness and introspection, extends through open and courageous conversations, and culminates in celebrating our shared humanity. As architects of our destiny, we embrace the transformative power of our family's story. This story can shape a future built on unity, empathy, and respect for all.

17-2 A Legacy of Positive Change: The Transformed Family Tree's Enduring Impact

As the transformation of the family tree takes root and evolves, it becomes an enduring legacy—a powerful force for positive change that extends far beyond the confines of familial boundaries. The values of empathy, understanding, and inclusivity, sowed with love and nurtured through generations, leave an indelible mark on the world—an impact that ripples out, touching the lives of countless others and shaping the course of history.

In the tapestry of human existence, families play a crucial role as the building blocks of society. They are the nurturing grounds for values and beliefs, the sanctuaries of love and support, and the cradles of identity and character. As the transformation of the family tree spreads its branches, it fosters an environment where empathy and compassion flourish, nurturing individuals who are deeply attuned to the needs of others.

At the heart of this legacy lies empathy—the capacity to understand and share in the emotions and experiences of others. As family members grow up witnessing kindness in action, they learn the art of active listening, the value of being present for one another, and the importance of seeing the world through diverse perspectives. Empathy becomes a guiding principle in their interactions with friends, colleagues, and even strangers, fostering a culture of compassion in every sphere of life.

Understanding, too, is a crucial pillar of this transformative legacy. As family members engage in open and respectful conversations, they embrace the beauty of diversity within the family. This understanding transcends family dynamics and permeates society as the transformed family members extend this grace to people of different backgrounds and walks of life.

Inclusivity is a natural outcome of the transformation within the family tree. As members break down the walls of division and create a genuine connection, they foster an environment where everyone feels seen, heard, and valued. This spirit of inclusivity radiates outward, inspiring the transformed individuals to work toward building a world where everyone has a seat at the table, regardless of their race, gender, ethnicity, or social status.

The values instilled within the transformed family tree create a ripple effect that extends to future generations. Children raised in an atmosphere of love, empathy, and understanding grow into adults who carry these principles into their lives and relationships. As they, too, become architects of their destiny, they contribute to the collective movement of positive change in the world.

The transformed family tree becomes a beacon of hope and inspiration for others to navigate their own paths of growth and healing. As they witness the power of love to heal wounds, bridge divides, and build bridges of connection; they are encouraged to embark on their own journeys of transformation.

Beyond the immediate family, this legacy of positive change reaches out to communities and societies. The transformed individuals become catalysts for social progress, working towards a more just and compassionate world. They engage in acts of service, advocate for the marginalized, and strive to create a future where all people can flourish.

In conclusion, the transformation of the family tree holds the potential to leave an enduring legacy of positive change. As empathy, understanding, and inclusivity permeate the fabric of family life, they become the guiding principles for future generations. The ripple effect of this transformative journey extends outward, transcending familial boundaries and touching the lives of countless others. This powerful force for positive change inspires the world to embrace a future built on love, compassion, and unity. As architects of our destiny, we assume the responsibility and privilege of nurturing a family tree that leaves an indelible mark on the world—an impact that uplifts, unites, and fosters a brighter tomorrow for all.

17-3 Rooted on Four Solid Unbendable Pillars

In the transformation journey, a family tree becomes a testament to the power of love, understanding, and compassion. This transformed family tree stands tall and strong, firmly rooted on a foundation supported by four solid unbendable pillars. These pillars are the guiding principles that shape the family's identity and define their collective legacy.

Love: At the core of the transformed family tree lies an abundance of love that knows no bounds and embraces each member unconditionally. This love is not merely an emotion but a conscious choice celebrating each family member's uniqueness, supporting them through trials and triumphs, and offering a haven where they can always find solace.

Love within the transformed family tree transcends differences and conflicts, healing wounds and fostering reconciliation. It forms the bedrock upon which trust and connection are built, creating a nurturing environment where each individual feels valued and cherished.

Understanding: The second pillar of the transformed family tree is understanding—the ability to listen with an open heart and to seek to comprehend the perspectives and experiences of one another. Knowledge nurtures empathy, allowing family members to step into each other's shoes and gain insights into the complexities of their lives.

Through understanding, the family cultivates a culture of communication and authentic dialogue. It creates space for constructive conversations, where diverse viewpoints are respected, and consensus sought. This pillar enables the family to overcome challenges, united by the knowledge that they are stronger together.

Respect: Respect is the third unbendable pillar of the transformed family tree. This pillar acknowledges each family member's inherent worth and dignity, fostering an environment where mutual respect prevails. It encourages open-mindedness and discourages judgment, allowing family members to express themselves without fear of reproach.

Respect within the transformed family tree paves the way for autonomy and self-expression. It empowers individuals to pursue their passions and dreams, even if they differ from traditional expectations. This pillar creates a space where diverse perspectives are embraced, enriching the family's collective wisdom.

Forgiveness: The fourth and final pillar that bolsters the transformed family tree is forgiveness—a willingness to let go of past grievances and extend compassion to oneself and others. Forgiveness is a healing force that liberates the family from grudges, paving the way for reconciliation and growth.

Through forgiveness, the transformed family tree breaks free from bitterness and resentment. Family members learn to navigate conflicts with grace and offer humility and apologies. This pillar fosters an atmosphere of emotional safety, where vulnerability is met with understanding and grace.

As the transformed family tree stands on these four solid unbendable pillars, it becomes a sanctuary of love, understanding, respect, and forgiveness. It is a source of strength, nurturing family members to thrive as individuals and as a cohesive unit. These pillars' values transcend generations, leaving an enduring legacy for the future.

The transformed family tree's influence reaches beyond the home's walls, impacting the larger community and society. It radiates the principles of compassion and unity, inspiring others to embark on their transformation journeys. The family becomes a beacon of hope, demonstrating that through love and understanding, families can break down barriers, heal wounds, and foster a world where everyone is seen, heard, and valued.

In conclusion, the transformed family tree stands tall on its foundation of four solid unbendable pillars—love, understanding, respect, and forgiveness. These pillars weave together the tapestry of a family that thrives on unity and compassion. As architects of our destiny, we embrace the responsibility of nurturing a transformed family tree that leaves a legacy of positive change, shaping not only the lives of its members but also the world they touch.

17-4 Embracing Unity Beyond Fake Tribes

In the journey of transformation, the family tree becomes a symbol of unity and compassion, transcending past divisions. By embracing a new era of understanding and reconciliation, the transformed family tree stands tall, firmly rooted on a foundation supported by four pillars—**Hutu, Tutsi, Sangwabutaka (Twa), and Ganwa;** the so-called **"fake tribes"** that once fueled hatred and conflict in Burundi.

Hutu: The first pillar of the transformed family tree is Hutu. This name was a term to categorize one group of people in Burundi, perpetuating division, and hate. In the transformed family tree, Hutu represents a willingness to shed the labels that separate us and to see beyond surface differences. It is a call to recognize our shared humanity and celebrate the family's diversity.

Hutu within the transformed family tree signifies unity, with family members embracing the notion that they are part of the same human family, regardless of historical labels or social constructs. Through the spirit of Hutu, the family tree becomes a testament to the power of love and acceptance, breaking down the walls of division and embracing each member as an integral part of the family's story.

Tutsi: The second pillar of the transformed family tree is Tutsi. This name once defined another group in Burundi, perpetuating a sense of "us" versus "them." Tutsi represents the journey toward reconciliation and healing in the transformed family tree. It is an invitation to extend forgiveness and empathy to those who may have been on different sides of historical conflicts.

Tutsi within the transformed family tree signifies understanding, where family members actively seek to comprehend the experiences and perspectives of one another. It fosters an environment of open communication and dialogue, allowing for constructive conversations that promote mutual respect and growth.

Twa (Abasangwabutaka): The third pillar of the transformed family tree is Twa—a term that once represented another group in Burundi, often marginalized and overlooked. In the transformed family tree, Twa represents the commitment to inclusivity and embracing the unique contributions of every family member.

Twa within the transformed family tree symbolizes respect, where everyone's worth and dignity are honored and celebrated. It creates a space where diverse perspectives are embraced and cherished, enriching the family's collective wisdom and fostering a spirit of unity.

Ganwa: The fourth and final pillar that bolsters the transformed family tree is Ganwa—an acknowledgment that historical divisions and labels may have been artificially created and imposed. In the transformed family tree, Ganwa represents the choice to break free from the past's chains and create a new narrative based on love and compassion.

Ganwa within the transformed family tree signifies forgiveness, where family members let go of past grievances and resentments, paving the way for reconciliation and healing. It fosters an atmosphere of emotional safety and vulnerability, where family members can extend grace and compassion to one another.

As the transformed family tree stands on these four pillars—Hutu, Tutsi, Twa, and Ganwa—it becomes a beacon of hope and inspiration for others. It demonstrates that families can overcome historical divisions through unity, understanding, respect, and forgiveness and build a future where love and compassion prevail.

The transformed family tree's influence extends beyond the home's boundaries, impacting the larger community and society. It radiates the principles of unity and reconciliation, inspiring others to embark on their transformation journeys. The family becomes a force for positive change, demonstrating that embracing our shared humanity can heal wounds, bridge divides, and create a world where all individuals are seen, heard, and valued.

In conclusion, the transformed family tree stands tall on its foundation of four pillars—Hutu, Tutsi, Twa, and Ganwa. These pillars represent unity, understanding, respect, and forgiveness, weaving together the tapestry of a family that thrives on love and compassion. As architects of our destiny, we embrace the responsibility of nurturing a transformed family tree that leaves a legacy of unity and reconciliation, shaping the lives of its members and the world they touch.   Through the power of transformation, the family tree becomes a testament to the strength of love and the human spirit. This testament reaches far beyond fake tribes and paves the way for a brighter and more inclusive tomorrow.

17-5 Clans in Burundi SAHUTUGA

Different clans such as ababanda, abajiji, abenengwe, abashubi, abanyakarama, abatare, abahanza, abahima, etc., have been integral parts of our rich tapestry of culture and heritage for generations. These clans represent related families with shared bloodlines, history, and traditions. They are the pillars of our social fabric, bearing unique customs and identities that contribute to the diverse mosaic of our nation.

In our transformed society, the social codes SA, HU, TU, and GA are significant and valuable, particularly within a clan and family framework. These codes reflect our ancestral ties, connecting us to our roots and grounding us in the traditions passed down through the ages.

While moving towards a more unified and harmonious nation with the SAHUTUGA concept, we must also cherish and protect the cultural diversity that has defined our clans. These clans' kinship and shared heritage bonds are sacred, and their customs and practices should remain untouched.

As we progress toward a future of greater unity, we must understand that the social codes of SA, HU, TU, and GA matter deeply within these close-knit groups. They are the threads that weave the fabric of our family and clan. These codes serve as a source of pride, guiding principles, and the foundation upon which the unique traditions of each clan are built.

We must respect and preserve the cultural wealth found within these clans. They are a testament to the enduring spirit of our people, a living connection to our ancestors, and a source of strength as we move forward on this transformative journey.

The social codes are not divisive but symbolic of the tapestry of identities that make up our nation. They are a testament to our diversity and the richness of our culture. As we embark on the path towards unity, we understand that while we are all Burundian SAHUTUGA, we also celebrate and honor the heritage and customs unique to each clan and family. This respect for our shared past and the beauty of our various traditions will strengthen our unity and propel us toward a brighter future.

CHAPTER 18

OUR NATION'S FAMILY NAME: SAHUTUGA

18-1 Embracing Our Transformed Nation: Burundi SAHUTUGA

In the grand tapestry of nations, names carry profound significance. They encapsulate the essence of a country's history, culture, and aspirations. Today, as we embark on a transformative journey, we proudly unveil the new identity of our beloved nation—**Burundi SAHUTUGA.**

The name SAHUTUGA transcends mere letters; it carries within it the unity we seek, the diversity we celebrate, and the legacy we intend to build. **SAHUTUGA, as the family name of our country, speaks to a profound shift in mindset—a shift from division to unity, from conflict to harmony, from isolation to inclusion.**

The components of SAHUTUGA—SA for Sangwabu-taka (Twa), HU for Hutu, TU for Tutsi, and GA for Ganwa —represent the threads that have woven our history. They embody the collective strength of our past while pointing toward a united future. Each letter is a tribute to the unique identities that have shaped our society, a testament to the bonds that tie us together as citizens of this great nation.

With Burundi SAHUTUGA, we boldly step forward in reshaping our national narrative. We shed the labels that once divided us and embrace a shared heritage that unites us. This new name signifies an end to the bitter past conflicts and heralds the beginning of a new era characterized by cooperation, mutual respect, and collaboration.

As Burundian SAHUTUGA, we are a beacon of hope for other nations struggling with similar challenges. Our journey toward unity and transformation exemplifies what is possible when a country collectively rises above its past and forge a new path.

Every citizen has a role to play in making the vision of Burundi SAHUTUGA a reality. By understanding the significance of this name, we take on the responsibility of nurturing a society that cherishes its diversity, empowers its citizens, and places unity at the forefront of its endeavors.

Burundi SAHUTUGA is not just a name but a declaration of our commitment to building a better future. It is a promise to our children and grandchildren that they will inherit a nation marked by progress, peace, and prosperity.

May this new name, Burundi SAHUTUGA, constantly re-mind us of our shared aspirations and catalyze the transformation we seek. Together, let us forge ahead, united under this banner of hope and promise, working tirelessly to create a nation we can all be proud of.

18-2 Unity in Diversity: The Power of a Transformed Nation's Name

In pursuing national unity and healing, a transformative approach to crafting the name of a nation can hold profound significance. **By combining the names of the four pillars— Sangwabutaka, Hutu, Tutsi, and Ganwa into SAHUTUGA as a unified name, the nation sets the stage for a decisive shift in citizens' minds and attitudes.** This innovative naming process symbolizes the nation's commitment to embracing diversity, fostering inclusivity, and healing historical wounds.

Combining the four pillars' names into one name signifies a collective recognition of the interconnectedness of the nation's people. It serves as a reminder that despite historical divisions, they are all part of the same tapestry—a tapestry woven with threads of different colors and textures, creating a vibrant and diverse whole.

This new nation's name reflects unity in diversity—a testament to the strength of embracing and leveraging differences as a source of collective power. It communicates a clear message to citizens and the international community that this nation is committed to building a future founded on understanding, respect, and cooperation.

For citizens, the transformation of the nation's name can catalyze a change of mindset. It invites them to see beyond the confines of historical divisions, encouraging them to view each other as fellow citizens bound by a shared destiny. By embracing this unified name, citizens shed the burdens of past conflicts and stereotypes and redefine their identity as a united people. **The power of a transformed nation's name lies in its ability to ignite a sense of pride and belonging among citizens.** It fosters a collective identity that transcends individual differences and fosters a shared sense of ownership and responsibility for the nation's future. Citizens are inspired to work together towards common goals, building bridges of cooperation and understanding beyond tribal affiliations.

Furthermore, the transformed nation's name becomes a hope for future generations. It communicates the nation's commitment to learning from past mistakes and building a society based on inclusivity, justice, and reconciliation. This name becomes a legacy of unity, peace, and progress that future generations can carry forward with pride and purpose.

Internationally, the transformation of the nation's name sends a powerful message of progress and resilience. It demonstrates that the country is on a transformative path, actively addressing historical wounds and working towards a brighter future. This change can garner support and recognition from the global community, opening doors for collaboration and positive engagement.

However, it is essential to acknowledge that transforming the nation's name is the beginning of a much deeper and more comprehensive process. The actual change lies in the nation's actions and policies to promote unity, justice, and equality among its citizens. The name serves as a symbolic representation of this commitment, but genuine transformation requires ongoing efforts at all levels of society.

In conclusion, combining the names of the four pillars—Sangwabutaka, Hutu, Tutsi, and Ganwa—into a single and unified name can transform citizens' minds. It signifies a commitment to unity in diversity, healing historical wounds, and building a future based on understanding and cooperation. This nation's name becomes a powerful emblem of collective pride, inspiring citizens to embrace a shared identity and work together for a brighter tomorrow. The nation seizes the opportunity to shape a legacy that transcends tribal affiliations—a legacy of unity, peace, and progress that will resonate for generations.

18-3 A Beacon of Hope: The Transformed Nation's Name as a Legacy for Future Generations

The transformation of a nation's name goes beyond a mere change in terminology; it becomes a powerful symbol—a beacon of hope shining brightly across the horizons of time. As the nation embraces a new identity, it communicates a profound commitment to learning from past mistakes and forging a path of inclusivity, justice, and reconciliation. This name becomes a legacy of unity, peace, and progress that future generations can carry forward with pride and purpose.

In the tapestry of history, nations bear the weight of their past—a narrative woven with both triumphs and tribulations. The transformed nation's name represents a pivotal moment—a turning point—where a country chooses to rise above its past, acknowledging the pain and suffering, and determining to chart a new course toward a brighter and more united future.

The beacon of hope radiates with the promise of progress. It signals to future generations that their ancestors took courageous steps to create a society that celebrates diversity, champions justice, and embraces reconciliation. This name inspires future citizens to build upon the foundations laid before them and carry the torch of positive change forward.

As future generations inherit this legacy, they are profoundly responsible for upholding the values that the transformed nation's name represents. It becomes a compass guiding them through the complexities of society, guiding their actions with the principles of inclusivity and empathy.

The legacy of unity embodied in the nation's name fosters a sense of belonging among future citizens. It creates a shared identity, transcending individual differences, tribal affiliations, and historical divisions. Future generations will forge relationships founded on understanding and respect, working together toward a common purpose—the prosperity and well-being of the nation and its people.

The beacon of hope also signifies a commitment to justice. It reminds future citizens that the nation's transformation goes beyond symbolic gestures; it requires a steadfast dedication to addressing historical injustices and creating a fair and equitable society. Future generations will be responsible for advocating for the marginalized and ensuring that everyone enjoys equal opportunities.

Furthermore, the transformed nation's name carries the promise of reconciliation. It acknowledges the wounds of the past and the need to heal deep-seated divisions. Future citizens are encouraged to engage in dialogue, listen with open hearts, and extend forgiveness to foster unity and understanding.

As the years turn into decades and the decades into centuries, the transformed nation's name endures as a beacon of hope and a source of inspiration. It serves as a reminder that positive change is not a fleeting moment, but an enduring commitment passed down from generation to generation.

Future generations are encouraged to tackle challenges while strengthening unity, peace, and progress. They must embrace the spirit of innovation and adaptability, seeking solutions to complex issues in an ever-changing world.

The transformed nation's name becomes a compass guiding the future in times of uncertainty and leading them toward paths of wisdom and compassion. It becomes a rallying cry for collective action, inspiring citizens to work together to overcome obstacles and build a society where every voice counts, and everyone is valued.

In conclusion, the transformed nation's name is a testament to hope's enduring power. It signifies a commitment to learning from the past and a determination to build a future based on inclusivity, justice, and reconciliation. This name becomes a legacy of unity, peace, and progress that future generations inherit with pride and purpose. As architects of our destiny, we embrace the responsibility to create a legacy that inspires hope and positive change for future generations. By infusing our actions with empathy and understanding, we shape a future where the beacon of hope shines brightly, illuminating the way toward a world where unity prevails and lasting peace flourishes.

CHAPTER 19

WEAVING THE SYMPHONY OF LOVE

19-1 A Legacy of Compassion, Kindness, and Empathy

Together, hand in hand, heart to heart, the family embarks on a timeless journey that transcends individual lifetimes and shapes the very fabric of history. In the tapestry of life, family members weave a remarkable story of compassion, kindness, and empathy—a symphony of love that resonates through the ages, touching hearts and minds far beyond the boundaries of time.

The transformation of a society is an intricate and profound process, and its roots lie within the family—the fundamental building block of any community. **Within the confines of a family, individuals are born with different "social codes," Sangwabutaka, Hutu, Tutsi, or Ganwa, based on the month they were born.** However, as we embark on a journey of healing and progress, the family emerges as the catalyst for embracing unity beyond these tribal affiliations, nurturing a society founded on empathy, understanding, and mutual respect.

  At the heart of this family's legacy lies a profound realization—the accurate measure of wealth is not found in material possessions but in the immeasurable virtues passed down from generation to generation. In this ageless pursuit, the family discovers its essence, its purpose—to nurture a bond built on love, understanding, and mutual support, creating a ripple effect that reverberates across generations.

Compassion, like a guiding star, illuminates the family's path. With each act of empathy and tenderness, family members bridge the gap between hearts, extending a hand of warmth and understanding. They embrace one another's joys and sorrows, weaving a web of interconnectedness that cradles each soul in a cocoon of comfort and belonging.

Kindness blossoms like a glorious flower in the garden of the family's heart. Each gentle word, each small gesture of care, paints a vivid canvas of love and thoughtfulness. The family members cultivate an atmosphere where every member feels cherished, seen, and valued—where judgment finds no place, and acceptance becomes the anthem that unites them.

Empathy, the harmonizing chord, lends rhythm to the family symphony. They listen to one another's stories, fears, and dreams through open ears and hearts. They embrace differences, knowing that within the tapestry of diversity lies the harmony of unity. Empathy binds them in an unbreakable bond, transcending temporal, or spatial distance.

As this symphony of love resounds, its melody echoes across generations. Each note the ancestors play guides the next generation's hand, passing down the treasured knowledge of love's profound impact. As the family embraces its young ones, it imparts not only worldly wisdom but also the wisdom of the heart—the enduring legacy of compassion, kindness, and empathy.

In this timeless tale, the family becomes a sanctuary where the warmth of love melts away the chill of life's hardships. It becomes a haven where children learn the art of loving, discover the strength in vulnerability, and find the courage to become their most authentic selves.

The family's legacy extends far beyond its borders, touching the lives of countless others. The ripples of compassion, kindness, and empathy reach the world, inspiring acts of goodness and benevolence that shape history. In these small acts, the family's symphony of love intertwines with the grand symphony of humanity, harmonizing with the universal melody of goodwill.

And so, as the family weaves its symphony of love, it embraces its divine purpose—planting seeds that transcend time and space. As the virtuous cycle unfolds, each generation becomes the gardener, tending to the roots with love and care, ensuring that the legacy of compassion, kindness, and empathy endures for all eternity.

In this beautiful tale of love and understanding, the family finds its eternal dance that transcends the boundaries of life and death. For in the hearts of those who cherish its melody, the family's symphony lives on, forever echoing in the annals of history, as a testament to the enduring power of love.

Together, hand in hand, heart to heart, the family weaves its symphony of compassion, kindness, and empathy—a melody that spans generations and shapes the course of history. As the baton passes from generation to generation, may each family member play their part, leaving a legacy of love etched into the hearts of all who come after them.

19-2 A Tapestry of Impact: The Family's Legacy Beyond Borders

In the vast tapestry of life, a family's legacy extends far beyond the boundaries of its home, weaving threads of influence that touch the lives of countless others. Like a stone cast into a still pond, the actions, values, and virtues cultivated within the family radiate outward, creating ripples of impact that reach far and wide.

The family's legacy is not confined to the walls of its dwelling but extends into the communities it touches. As family members embody compassion, kindness, and empathy in their daily interactions, their positive energy ripples through their neighborhoods. They become beacons of light, illuminating the paths of others, and offering solace and support in times of need.

The seeds of love sown within the family take root in society, blossoming into acts of altruism and service. The children, raised in an environment of care and consideration, carry the torch of compassion forward, becoming the change agents that uplift those around them. Through their deeds, they become catalysts for positive change, creating a ripple effect that extends far beyond the family's reach.

In the workplace, family members carry the ethos of empathy and understanding, fostering a culture of collaboration and mutual respect. Their ability to see beyond differences and embrace diverse perspectives allows harmonious relationships with colleagues and clients. The family's legacy becomes a force that transforms corporate environments into compassionate and inclusive spaces.

As family members engage in civic life, they become agents of change in their communities. Their dedication to serving others, inspired by the values instilled in the family, leads to the establishment of community projects, social initiatives, and philanthropic endeavors. Their actions resonate with others, igniting a spirit of giving and a desire to impact society positively.

The family's legacy weaves a thread of hope and resilience, especially in times of adversity. Their ability to weather challenges with unity and love inspires others facing their trials. The strength they draw from their interconnectedness becomes a model for communities to unite and support one another in times of need.

The impact extends to future generations through the seeds of compassion, kindness, and empathy planted within the family. As the family nurtures these virtues, they pass on values and a sense of responsibility—a responsibility to make the world a better place, one act of kindness at a time.

Beyond the local community, the family's legacy can potentially touch lives globally. The values of empathy and compassion ripple through social media and other digital platforms, influencing hearts and minds across borders. Their online presence becomes a platform for spreading positivity and promoting understanding on a global scale.

The family's legacy becomes part of the collective human story—a narrative of love and understanding that transcends geographical boundaries and cultural differences. Their contribution to building a more compassionate world becomes a timeless tale—a legacy that reverberates throughout the ages.

In the grand tapestry of life, the family's legacy intertwines with the stories of countless others. Their impact reaches places they may never physically venture, leaving an imprint on the hearts and souls of people they may never meet. The family's symphony of compassion, kindness, and empathy becomes a universal melody, resonating with the shared humanity that binds us.

As the family weaves its tapestry of impact, it discovers the true essence of its purpose not to make a difference within its own sphere but in the lives of all humanity. Each act of love, each display of understanding, and each gesture of empathy creates a chain reaction of positive change—a ripple effect that touches lives far and wide.

In this realization, the family becomes a force for good —an agent of transformation that leaves an indelible mark on the world. As their legacy extends far beyond borders, they become living proof of the profound power of love, compassion, and empathy to shape history. Together, hand in hand, heart to heart, the family stands as a testament to the enduring impact of values that transcend time and space—a testament to the infinite potential of the human spirit.

CHAPTER 20

FROM FAMILY UNITY TO SOCIETAL HARMONY

20-1 Embracing Diversity and Healing Historical Divisions

The transformation of a society is an intricate and profound process, and its roots lie within the family—the fundamental building block of any community. **Within the confines of a family, individuals are born with different "social codes," like Sangwabutaka, Hutu, Tutsi, or Ganwa, based on the month they were born.** However, as we embark on a journey of healing and progress, the family emerges as the catalyst for embracing unity beyond these tribal affiliations, nurturing a society founded on empathy, understanding, and mutual respect.

A Tapestry of Diversity: The family, with its members identified with various "social codes," represents a tapestry of diversity—a mosaic of experiences, cultures, and traditions. By acknowledging and celebrating this diversity, the family sets the stage for a transformation that values and cherishes everyone's uniqueness.

Within the family, members learn to appreciate the richness of different backgrounds and experiences. This appreciation becomes the cornerstone for embracing diversity within the broader society, fostering an environment where everyone's voice is heard and valued.

Healing Historical Wounds: The family acts as an incubator for healing historical wounds that have divided communities for generations. By confronting the pain and trauma of past conflicts, family members can initiate a process of reconciliation and forgiveness.

As empathy and understanding grow within the family unit, they become the bedrock for healing broader societal divisions. This healing process ripples outward, encouraging communities to confront their shared history and move towards a united future.

Empathy as the Bridge: Empathy is a powerful bridge that connects families who were once separated by "fake tribes." As they take the time to listen and understand each other's experiences, they develop a deeper connection built on compassion and shared humanity.

This bridge of empathy extends beyond the family's boundaries, fostering connections between different communities within the society. As more families embrace compassion, the nation's fabric comes back together, creating a network of understanding and support.

Mutual Respect and Inclusivity: Within the family, mutual respect and inclusivity become guiding principles. Members learn to treat each other with dignity, regardless of their affiliations. This culture of care becomes the foundation for a society where everyone is treated fairly and equally.

As the family extends these principles to interactions with the broader community, they transform societal norms. Inclusivity becomes the norm, transcending tribal barriers and enabling each citizen to participate fully in the nation's development.

Leading by Example: The transformation within the family is a living example for the community to follow. As they journey towards unity and understanding, the family inspires others to do the same.

Their commitment to positive change shines as a beacon of hope, encouraging other families to embark on their transformational journeys. As more families lead by example, the cumulative effect is a society embracing unity and progress.

Educating Future Generations: The transformation within the family has a lasting impact on future generations. Children raised in an environment of unity and empathy grow up with a profound sense of belonging and responsibility towards their community.

As they mature into active members of society, they carry the values learned within their families, serving as agents of change, and advocating for a harmonious society. This intergenerational transfer of values ensures the sustainability of transformation across time.

In conclusion, the family is the bedrock of societal transformation, a microcosm of the broader community. Within its loving embrace, members historically identified with different "fake tribes" learn to embrace unity beyond these divisions. Empathy, healing, mutual respect, and inclusivity become guiding principles that extend beyond the family unit, nurturing a society of diversity, understanding, and mutual respect.

As architects of our destiny, we recognize the family's pivotal role in shaping our society's transformation. By fostering a culture of unity and healing historical divisions, the family catalyzes a brighter future—a future where they celebrate diversity, abundant empathy, and societal harmony reigns sup.

20-2. Emphasizing Empathy and Understanding

At the heart of the values education program lies a focus on empathy and understanding. Students are encouraged to listen actively to others' perspectives, consider different viewpoints, and embrace diversity with an open mind.

Students learn to empathize with others' experiences and emotions through role-playing exercises, storytelling, and real-life examples. This process fosters a sense of shared humanity, breaking down barriers of misunderstanding and encouraging students to treat each other with kindness and respect.

Promoting Inclusivity and Respect: The program should encourage inclusivity and respect for all school community members. By organizing events celebrating various cultures, traditions, and identities, students gain a deeper appreciation for the richness of diversity.

Activities that encourage teamwork, cooperation, and collaboration further reinforce the value of mutual respect. These experiences empower students to become ambassadors for inclusivity, nurturing a school environment where everyone feels valued and accepted.

Encouraging Civic Engagement: As students progress through the program, they are encouraged to implement their values through civic engagement initiatives. From community service projects to advocating for social causes, students learn the practical application of empathy and unity in positively impacting society.

Through these experiences, students become active participants in shaping the transformation of their communities, extending the values they have learned to the broader society.

Nurturing Responsible Citizenship: As students advance to higher grade levels, the program evolves to include discussions on responsible citizenship and ethical decision-making. Students explore complex societal issues, considering the consequences of their actions on others and the environment.

The program empowers students to become critical thinkers, encouraging them to be agents of positive change in their communities. By nurturing a sense of responsibility towards others and the world, the program equips students to carry the torch of transformation into adulthood.

In conclusion, the transformation within the family serves as a guiding light for the broader community, inspiring positive change from homes to different schools. By establishing a values education program from elementary school to high school, we create a continuum of learning that nurtures empathy, understanding, and mutual respect in young generations.

Through interactive and holistic approaches, students learn to celebrate diversity, embrace unity, and practice the

values that promote a harmonious society. As architects of our destiny, we recognize the significance of instilling these values in future citizens, ensuring that our transformational journey endures through the actions and attitudes of future generations. By cultivating a culture of empathy and respect in schools, we pave the way for a society where positive change is embraced and perpetuated by each successive generation.

20-3 Empowering Minds Through Education: Integrating Universal Rights and Unbendable Pillars

In the tapestry of our transformed nation, education is not just a means to acquire knowledge; it is a cornerstone of unity and progress. We recognize that education has the power to shape not only individual lives but also the destiny of our entire nation. To further enhance this transformative journey, we are embarking on a strategy that will infuse the principles of unity, universal human rights, and our unwavering pillars into the very fabric of education.

Picture a classroom filled with eager young minds, each clutching a book that holds academic lessons and the essence of our nation's identity. As we turn the pages of this initiative, we envision incorporating the text of universal human rights and the core principles of our four unbendable pillars of Burundi SAHUTUGA into educational materials, ranging from textbooks to notebooks.

The reasoning behind this strategy is twofold: firstly, it serves as a perpetual reminder of the ideals we stand for as a nation, and secondly, it facilitates a cascading effect of

learning that extends beyond the confines of the classroom. As students engage with these texts, they internalize the values of unity, empathy, and respect, forming a deep connection with our transformed identity.

But the impact doesn't stop at the students. As these educational materials make their way into homes, the messages seep into the consciousness of parents, siblings, neighbors, and communities. The collective wisdom of our nation is shared and celebrated, fostering a sense of camaraderie that transcends generational boundaries.

Imagine parents discussing the values and principles outlined in these materials with their children. Picture neighbors gathering to read, understand, and reflect upon the universal human rights that bind us all as citizens of the world. This strategy transforms education into a unifying force that bridges the gap between generations and reinforces the foundations of our nation.

Through this initiative, we are making a deliberate effort to empower minds and hearts, instilling a sense of shared responsibility for our collective future. We are turning classrooms into spaces of inspiration, where every lesson extends beyond the curriculum to shape our identity as Burundi SAHUTUGA citizens.

As we embark on this journey, we understand that education is not just about memorizing facts; it's about internalizing values, igniting curiosity, and fostering critical thinking. By embedding universal human rights and our unbendable pillars within educational materials, we are sowing the seeds of a brighter future where unity, understanding, and progress flourish in the minds of our citizens.

In this way, education becomes a dynamic force that propels us forward, guiding us toward a future where the principles we hold dear are not just words on a page but living truths that shape our interactions, decisions, and destiny as a united and transformed nation.

20-4 Uniting Institutions for Identity Transformation: Workshops for a Harmonious Society

As the transformation journey towards a harmonious society continues, the collaboration of different institutions becomes pivotal in shaping a collective identity founded on empathy, understanding, and mutual respect. Institutions, such as the military force, religious groups, and governmental and non-governmental organizations, wield significant influence over society. These institutions can foster a culture of unity, acceptance, and positive change by organizing workshops centered around identity transformation, propelling the nation toward a more compassionate and inclusive future.

The Military Force: The military is crucial in safeguarding the nation's security. The military can strengthen its commitment to national unity and inclusivity by organizing workshops on identity transformation. Through these workshops, soldiers can understand the diverse backgrounds and experiences that comprise the nation they protect.

By fostering empathy and cultural awareness, the military force can build bridges of understanding with the communities they serve. Such workshops also provide opportunities to address historical grievances and promote reconciliation between different groups, ultimately contributing to a more cohesive and peaceful society.

Religious Groups: Religious institutions are potent agents of influence within society, shaping the beliefs and values of their followers. Organizing workshops on identity transformation within religious communities encourages open dialogue and understanding.

Religious leaders can emphasize the common themes of compassion, love, and acceptance in their teachings, fostering an environment that transcends divisive tribal affiliations. Through these workshops, religious groups become advocates for unity, guiding their congregations towards building a society where the shared humanity is celebrated and upheld.

Governmental Institutions: Governmental institutions are responsible for crafting policies impacting society. By organizing workshops on identity transformation, these institutions can ensure that policies are framed through a lens of inclusivity and justice.

Government officials can learn about different communities' diverse needs and aspirations, making informed decisions that uplift marginalized groups. The workshops also provide an avenue for citizens to actively engage in policymaking, cultivating a sense of ownership and empowerment within the society.

Non-Governmental Organizations (NGOs): NGOs play a crucial role in advocating for the rights of marginalized communities and driving social change. By organizing workshops on identity transformation, NGOs can provide a platform for diverse voices to be heard.

These workshops equip individuals with the tools to address discrimination, promote social cohesion, and advocate for the rights of all citizens. The collective efforts of NGOs united through the shared vision of a transformed society, have the potential to influence broader societal attitudes and policies.

Collaborative Efforts: The success of identity transformation workshops lies in collaborative efforts between different institutions. Joint workshops involving military forces, religious groups, and governmental and non-governmental organizations create a space for meaningful dialogue and mutual understanding.

Collaboration between these institutions fosters a comprehensive approach to societal transformation, ensuring that unity and acceptance resonate across various spheres of influence.

Measuring Impact and Sustainability: As the workshops progress, measuring their impact and sustainability is essential. Regular evaluations and feedback loops help refine the workshop content and approach, effectively conveying the transformative messages.

Long-term sustainability is achieved through incorporating the principles of identity transformation into the institutional fabric of each participating organization. This includes integrating empathy and inclusivity into training programs, policies, and decision-making processes.

In conclusion, different institutions—military forces, religious groups, governmental and non-governmental organizations—significantly influence society's beliefs and values. These institutions contribute to developing a compassionate and inclusive community by organizing workshops centered around identity transformation.

Through empathy, understanding, and mutual respect fostered in these workshops, a culture of unity and positive change emerges. Collaborative efforts between institutions build bridges of understanding, creating a ripple effect that extends to every corner of society. As architects of our destiny, we recognize that the collective transformation achieved through these workshops will pave the way for a nation where unity prevails, and societal harmony becomes the bedrock of progress.

CHAPTER 21

EMBRACING GLOBAL CITIZENSHIP

21-1 Dual Citizenship in Burundi SAHUTUGA

In the realm of our transformed nation, the horizons of opportunity stretch far beyond our borders. Burundi SAHUTUGA welcomes an era of open-mindedness, where the world becomes our canvas, and every citizen is an artist free to paint their life's journey.

In recognition of this spirit of exploration and the evolving nature of our globalized world, we will proudly offer the privilege of dual citizenship to every individual within our nation's embrace. **This policy reflects our commitment to empowering our citizens with the freedom to explore, dream, and contribute locally and internationally.** By holding citizenship in more than one country, our citizens can access a broader range of opportunities, whether seeking education, employment, or a new experience. It is a testament to our belief that diversity enriches us all and that cross-cultural interactions enhance our collective wisdom.

Dual citizenship means that Burundi SAHUTUGA citizens can retain their original citizenship while acquiring another from a different country. This allows for seamless movement across borders, access to educational institutions and job markets in multiple nations, and the ability to engage with the global community fully. It is a recognition that geographical boundaries do not confine our citizens; instead, they are free to explore the world as ambassadors of our transformed nation.

The policy of dual citizenship is not just a legal framework; it's an embodiment of our vision for a progressive and interconnected society. It encourages citizens to embrace the world with an open heart, collaborate, learn, and contribute to the global human experience. It affirms our belief that Burundi SAHUTUGA is not an isolated entity but an integral part of the tapestry of nations.

As we chart our course toward a prosperous future, we do so with the understanding that our citizens' diverse experiences, acquired from their journeys near and far, will enrich our nation's growth. By granting the privilege of double citizenship, we are extending an invitation for our people to be active participants in shaping the course of the world.

Burundi SAHUTUGA's embrace of dual citizenship marks a significant stride toward a more inclusive, interconnected, and forward-looking nation. Let us seize this opportunity to explore the world and share the values and virtues

166 - AUDACE MPOZIRINIGA

of our transformed identity, contributing to the betterment of humanity on a global scale.

21-2 Extending our Transformed Identity: Inviting the International Community to Embrace Our Nation's Transformation

In the quest for progress and international support, one innovative approach is offering the international community a unique opportunity—to carry our transformed identity once they enter our nation temporarily. By extending this invitation, we welcome global citizens to embrace and experience the profound changes that have shaped our society. This act fosters mutual understanding and demonstrates the sincerity of our transformation efforts, making a compelling case for international support and cooperation.

The Essence of Transformed Identity: Our transformed identity is a testament to the resilience of our nation—a journey of healing, unity, and reconciliation. It embodies the values of empathy, inclusivity, and justice that have guided our transformation process. By offering the international community a temporary chance to carry this identity, we extend an open invitation to engage with the essence of our nation's progress.

Fostering Empathy and Understanding: As global citizens temporarily embrace our transformed identity; they gain unique insights into the challenges and triumphs that have shaped our history. By immersing themselves in our transformed society, they foster empathy and understanding, transcending historical narratives and stereotypes that might have once divided us.

This experiential exchange encourages a deeper appreciation for the transformative power of unity and compassion. The international community can witness the tangible results of our efforts towards inclusivity and justice, inspiring collaboration, and solidarity.

A Shared Journey: The international community becomes integral to our shared journey by temporarily carrying our transformed identity. They contribute to the narrative of positive change and lend their voices to the chorus of progress. This shared experience fosters a sense of interconnectedness, where global citizens recognize that our transformation resonates with broader aspirations for a better world.

Amplifying the Call for Support: Offering our transformed identity to the international community amplifies our call for support. It showcases our commitment to an open and inclusive society, strengthening our case for cooperation and assistance. International partners, witnessing our dedication to unity and peace, are more likely to be inspired to extend their support and collaboration.

A Platform for Dialogue and Exchange: Temporarily carrying our transformed identity creates a platform for meaningful dialogue and exchange. It enables global citizens to share their perspectives and experiences, fostering an enriching cultural interchange that transcends borders. This exchange of ideas and values encourages collaboration on shared challenges, leading to innovative solutions and mutual growth.

Shaping a Global Movement: Our invitation to carry our transformed identity temporarily has the potential to spark a global movement for positive change. As international partners experience the transformative power of unity and empathy, we may inspire some people to replicate similar efforts in their nations.

This global movement can become a force for collective progress, where nations collaborate to address shared challenges such as inequality, conflict resolution, and environmental sustainability.

In conclusion, extending our transformed identity to the international community is a powerful way to call for their support and cooperation. By immersing themselves in our nation's journey of healing and progress, global citizens can foster empathy, understanding, and solidarity. This act catalyzes dialogue, collaboration, and the formation of a global movement for positive change.

As architects of our destiny, we recognize the value of inviting the international community to embrace a transformed society built on inclusivity and justice. Together, hand in hand, heart to heart, we can forge a more harmonious world where unity and compassion reign supreme, breaking down barriers and paving the way for a brighter future for all.

CHAPTER 22

GOOD GOVERNANCE

Establishing transparent, accountable, and inclusive governance structures is crucial for development. Good governance involves promoting the rule of law, combating corruption, and ensuring effective public administration. Good governance builds trust, attracts investment, and enables efficient resource allocation.

22-1 A Call for Mutual Respect and Efficient Governance

In the cadence of time, moments are the currency of progress—a treasure that, once squandered, cannot be reclaimed. Our transformed nation's journey toward prosperity hinges on our ability to redeem time to cast aside needless distractions and unfocused endeavors. This chapter is a resounding call to action, urging us to reevaluate our priorities, streamline our efforts, and forge a harmonious relationship between governance and spirituality.

A New Dawn of Efficiency: In our pursuit of progress, we are called to cast off the shackles of inefficiency. With a renewed sense of purpose, we turn our gaze to the hours lost in meandering politico-religious meetings. While unity and dialogue are integral to our identity, we must recognize the urgency of channeling our energies into more constructive avenues that yield tangible results for our citizens.

Mapping Out Productive Pathways: The redemption of time is not merely a concept but a blueprint for efficiency. It beckons us to devise strategic plans synchronizing government programs and individual initiatives, ensuring our collective efforts march harmoniously toward our shared goals. Weekdays, reserved for focused pursuits, hold the potential to unfurl new horizons of progress, while weekends become sacred grounds for ceremonies and religious gatherings that uplift our spirits.

Honoring Both Caesar and God: The timeless wisdom of the age's echoes through the corridors of history—**"Give back to Caesar what is Caesar's and to God what is God's."** This scriptural guidance reverberates with relevance in our contemporary context, reminding us to allocate our energies wisely. By discerning the rightful domains of governance and spirituality, we ensure that both are served with the due reverence they deserve.

Fostering Unity Through Respect: By giving due respect to religion and politics, we forge a path of unity. As citizens who aspire to heal divisions, we recognize that both these realms possess the potential to nurture our transformed nation. Politics is the key to governance, administration, and progress, while religion is a guiding light for ethics, values, and spirituality.

A Unified Path Forward: As we reconcile the threads of time, weaving them into a unified tapestry, we shape a future guided by purpose, respect, and shared aspirations. In the symphony of transformation, every moment counts. By judiciously allocating our time by separating and valuing our civic responsibilities and spiritual convictions, we orchestrate a melody of progress that resonates with the heartbeats of every citizen.

The Redemption of Time: A Collective Responsibility. Redeeming time is not merely a call to action for individuals but a collective responsibility woven into our nation's narrative. As we realign our priorities, let us heed the wisdom that time offers—time to build, grow, and harmonize. Through the unity of purpose and respect for earthly and spiritual pursuits, we redeem the hours, shaping a future that is not fragmented by unnecessary divisions but fortified by a shared vision of a transformed nation.

22-2 Independent Justice; The Bedrock of Good Governance

In the tapestry of a transformed nation, the threads of justice weave an essential pattern. Independent judge serves as the cornerstone of good governance, ensuring the equitable application of laws and safeguarding the rights and dignity of every citizen. As we aspire to establish a society founded on fairness and equality, we recognize that a robust legal framework and a profound understanding of the law are pivotal.

Empowering Citizens through Legal Literacy:

Our commitment to justice starts with the empowerment of our citizens. An informed populace is better equipped to navigate the intricacies of the legal landscape and contribute to preserving law and order. To this end, we are dedicated to enhancing legal literacy among our citizens. By providing accessible resources, educational programs, and community workshops, we strive to cultivate a society that not only comprehends but also respects the laws that govern it.

Access to Justice for All:

Our justice should be accessible to everyone, regardless of their financial circumstances. To this end, we are pioneering a groundbreaking initiative—free legal aid. We recognize that the inability to afford legal representation should never be a barrier to seeking justice. Through this program, those in need will have access to skilled legal professionals who advocate on their behalf, ensuring that justice is served equitably.

Preserving Dignity Through Fair Trials:

Central to our vision is the preservation of human dignity. Fair trials are not just a legal requirement; they are a testament to respect for the sanctity of every individual. Our judicial system will uphold the principles of due process, ensuring that the accused are given a fair chance to defend themselves. This commitment to fairness reflects our commitment to justice that safeguards the rights and dignity of all citizens.

Fostering Trust in the Legal System:

The pillars of a just society are trust and confidence in the legal system. As we lay the foundation for good governance, we are equally devoted to building a legal framework that is transparent, unbiased, and accountable. By promoting transparency in court proceedings, implementing safeguards against corruption, and ensuring that justice is served without prejudice, we aim to foster trust in our legal institutions.

A Journey Towards Accountability:

Justice extends beyond individual cases; it encompasses accountability at all levels. Our commitment to independent justice includes holding public officials accountable for their actions. Corruption, abuse of power, and misconduct will be thoroughly investigated through an impartial judiciary, ensuring that those entrusted with governance are answerable to the people they serve.

Conclusion: The Path to Equitable Governance

As the curtains rise on this chapter of our transformation, the spotlight shines on the vital role of independent justice in building a society founded on integrity and fairness. We recognize that a nation can only thrive when its legal system is robust, accessible, and just. By fostering legal literacy, providing free legal aid, and upholding the principles of transparency and accountability, we pave the way for equitable governance where every citizen stands confident in their rights and knows that justice will be served without bias or prejudice.

22-3 Eradicating Corruption: The Cornerstone of Good Governance

In the intricate tapestry of a transformed nation, the fight against corruption weaves a critical thread. As architects of a just society, we understand that corruption is a formidable adversary to good governance, undermining trust, justice, and progress. Our commitment to upholding justice is intrinsically tied to our unwavering determination to root out corruption from every corner of our nation.

Making Transparency shine:
Transparency stands as our most potent weapon against corruption. We recognize that a lack of transparency breeds fertile ground for corrupt practices to thrive. In our pursuit of justice, we are dedicated to implementing measures that ensure transparency at all levels of governance. By shedding light on processes, transactions, and decision-making, we lay the foundation for accountability and diminish the shadows where corruption hides.

Fighting Graft from the Roots:
Corruption takes many forms, from bribery and embezzlement to nepotism and cronyism. We recognize that combatting corruption requires comprehensive efforts. Our strategy includes:

- Strengthening anti-corruption laws.
- Enforcing stricter penalties for those engaged in corrupt practices.
- Creating avenues for whistleblowers to come forward without fear of retaliation.

By attacking corruption at its roots, we aim to create an environment where illicit practices wither and die.

Empowering Citizens to Say No to Corruption:
Citizens are the guardians of our nation's integrity. Empowering them to stand against corruption is pivotal in our quest for

justice. We are committed to launching extensive anti-corruption awareness campaigns that educate citizens about their rights and the corrosive effects of corruption. Through education and advocacy, we aim to create a groundswell of resistance to corruption, turning citizens into active participants in the fight for justice.

Ensuring Accountability Across the Board:

A just society demands accountability from its leaders. We acknowledge that corruption can permeate even the highest echelons of power. Our commitment to justice includes holding public officials accountable for their actions. By establishing independent bodies for investigating and prosecuting corruption cases, we ensure that those who abuse their positions of authority are held answerable under the law.

A Vision of a Corruption-Free Nation:

Our vision extends beyond eradicating corruption; it encompasses the creation of a nation where transparency, integrity, and justice are paramount. We envision a society where pursuing personal gain at the expense of the common good is not tolerated. Our fight against corruption is not merely a slogan but a relentless commitment to forging a future where our nation's resources are used for the collective benefit and public trust is restored.

Conclusion: The Battle for Justice

As we close this chapter in our journey toward transformation, our focus remains unwavering—the battle against corruption. By shining a light on transparency, empowering citizens, and enforcing accountability, we construct a bulwark against corruption's insidious influence. Our dedication to justice is a testament to our resolve to forge a society free from the chains of corruption, where every citizen can trust in the fairness of governance and the promise of a brighter future.

CHAPTER 23

MERITOCRACY

Meritocracy is a system where individuals advance and gain opportunities based on their merits, typically determined by their skills, abilities, and achievements rather than factors like social status, wealth, or personal connections. In a meritocracy, the emphasis is on rewarding and promoting individuals who demonstrate excellence and competence in their respective fields, fostering a fair and level playing field for all members of society. This system aims to ensure that positions of influence and leadership are filled by those most capable of performing their roles effectively, regardless of other characteristics.

23-1 The Pillar of Equitable Opportunity

In the transformative tapestry of our nation, Burundi SAHUTUGA, the rise of a meritocratic society is not just an aspiration—it's a legacy of justice that reshapes the landscape of opportunity. Meritocracy emerges as the bedrock principle upon which we will every sector, industry, and institution. It is a testament to our commitment to fairness, a declaration that opportunities are granted based on capabilities rather than inherited privileges. This chapter delves into the profound impact of embracing meritocracy, a legacy of justice that upholds the principles of our transformed nation.

An Equal Playing Field. At the heart of meritocracy lies an equal playing field where individuals can excel and rise based solely on their abilities. In a society marked by meritocracy, the shackles of inherited privileges—whether political, regional, or family ties—are broken. This dismantling of barriers ensures that every citizen, regardless of background, is allowed to showcase their talents and contribute to the progress of our nation.

Merited, Not Inherited. In our transformed society, opportunities are not handed down like ancestral heirlooms; they are earned through dedication, competence, and unwavering commitment. The embrace of meritocracy asserts that positions of influence and responsibility are the outcome of hard work, perseverance, and a continuous pursuit of excellence. This ethos encourages citizens to strive for greatness, knowing their efforts will be rewarded based on merit.

A Thriving Ecosystem. As meritocracy flourishes, our nation's ecosystem transforms into a thriving landscape of innovation and collaboration. Individuals are empowered to contribute their unique perspectives, talents, and skills, fueling a creative spirit that propels industries forward. The dynamic interplay of ideas, fostered by a meritocratic culture, catalyzes breakthroughs, and accelerates our journey toward progress.

A Legacy of Justice. The legacy of meritocracy is rooted in justice. This justice ensures that positions of influence and leadership are occupied by individuals who have demonstrated their competence. This legacy extends beyond individual accomplishment; it infiltrates the collective consciousness, forging a society where fairness is the cornerstone. The principles of meritocracy ripple through generations, a gift to our successors that speaks of integrity, equality, and justice.

Unveiling Hidden Potential. Meritocracy is a revelation of hidden potential—a beacon that illuminates the path of those who may have been overlooked due to systemic inequalities. When opportunities are not confined by privilege, brilliance can emerge from the unlikeliest sources. This unveiling of untapped talent enhances our nation's capabilities, infusing every sector with fresh perspectives and new horizons.

A Bold Declaration. By embracing meritocracy, our transformed nation boldly declares that all citizen's contributions are valued, regardless of their background. It signals to the world that we are architects of a just society, where the legacy we build is one of fairness, equity, and advancement for all. It reaffirms our commitment to justice and empowers citizens to take charge of their destiny, knowing that their efforts will be acknowledged and rewarded.

A Future Forged by Merit. As we forge into a brighter future, meritocracy serves as our guiding light. It propels us toward a destiny where competence reigns supreme, opportunities are granted based on capability, and our transformed nation thrives through the collective brilliance of its citizens. Through the legacy of meritocracy, we weave a tapestry of justice, unity, and progress—an enduring testament to our identity as architects of a society that places fairness at its very core.

23-2 Pioneering Gender Equality: A Path to Progress
Pioneering Gender Equality: A Resolute Commitment

In the realm of our transformed nation, the principles of gender equality stand as pillars of progress. Guided by our unwavering commitment to justice and fairness, we are resolute in breaking down the barriers that have long impeded equal opportunities for all citizens, regardless of gender. The journey towards true gender equality requires a comprehensive approach that champions meritocracy while addressing historical imbalances.

Championing Meritocracy for All:

Meritocracy serves as the cornerstone of our commitment to gender equality. A rigorous adherence to merit-based principles will govern our institutions and employment sectors. We recognize that every individual, irrespective of their gender, brings unique skills and talents to the table. By promoting meritocracy, we ensure that the most qualified and capable individuals rise to positions of influence and responsibility, contributing to our nation's progress.

A Window of Opportunity:

While gender equality is non-negotiable, we acknowledge the need for nuanced strategies in certain instances. In some departments or sectors where historical gender imbalances persist, we understand that achieving immediate parity may require additional time. As such, we may accept a temporary window of up to 10% as we work diligently to address underlying systemic disparities. This approach allows us to balance our commitment to equality with the practical realities of our journey.

Empowering Through Education and Advocacy:

True gender equality transcends mere statistics; it embodies a cultural shift that celebrates diversity and inclusivity. We are dedicated to fostering an environment where individuals of all genders can thrive. This includes robust educational programs that dispel gender stereotypes, empower women and men alike, and encourage open dialogue about the importance of equality. Through advocacy and awareness campaigns, we intend to reshape societal norms, creating a future where every citizen is valued for their capabilities, not their gender.

Leadership and Representation:

Gender equality is not just about numbers; it's about representation. We recognize the importance of having diverse voices at decision-making tables. Our commitment to gender equality extends to leadership positions across industries and institutions. By elevating capable women and men to leadership roles, we ensure a balanced representation that reflects the diversity of our nation and contributes to well-informed and inclusive policies.

Conclusion: A Journey of Empowerment

As we conclude this chapter on gender equality, our determination remains steadfast. Our vision is clear: to create a transformed nation where opportunities are accessible to all, regardless of gender. Through the steadfast implementation of meritocracy and the gradual dismantling of historical gender imbalances, we pave the way for a society defined by its commitment to justice, progress, and the principles of equality. Gender equality isn't just a goal—it's an intrinsic part of our identity as architects of a just and equitable future.

23-3 Empowerment Through Knowledge: Transforming Employment Eligibility

In the heart of our transformed nation, Burundi SAHUTUGA, a paradigm shift that places knowledge at the forefront of employment eligibility emerges. The keys to opportunity are no longer shrouded in privilege or nepotism; they are earned through education, experience, and a commitment to continuous growth. This chapter delves into the transformative power of knowledge-based recruitment and promotion, shaping an empowered and equipped workforce to steer our nation toward unparalleled heights.

A Foundation of Excellence. Knowledge is the cornerstone upon which our transformed nation's workforce is built. Just as a solid foundation supports a towering structure, so does a foundation of knowledge underpin a resilient and prosperous society. Education, experience, and a demonstration of skills become the benchmarks against which individuals are measured, ensuring that every step of the employment journey is guided by merit and competence.

Education: The Beacon of Opportunity In our transformed nation, education becomes the beacon that illuminates the path to opportunity. Pursuing knowledge is not a luxury but a fundamental right that paves the way for individuals to unlock their potential and contribute meaningfully to their communities. By valuing education as a pillar of eligibility, we cultivate a culture of learning where every citizen can explore their passions, expand their horizons, and, ultimately, shape their destiny.

Experience: A Tapestry of Growth. The experience becomes a tapestry of growth woven through the fabric of everyone's journey. From entry-level positions to the pinnacle of leadership, the accumulation of experience fosters expertise, hones skills, and imparts a nuanced understanding of the industries and institutions that drive our nation forward. It's a testament to individuals' commitment and dedication to their craft, a testament that should not go unnoticed.

Tests of Proficiency: A Level Playing Field. Tests of proficiency serve as the great equalizer—a level playing field upon which all candidates can showcase their abilities. These assessments are not barriers; they are gateways to opportunity, allowing individuals to prove their competence and readiness for roles of significance. Whether through written examinations, practical demonstrations, or simulations, tests of proficiency ensure that all citizens, regardless of background, have the chance to demonstrate their potential.

Meritocracy: A Legacy of Justice. The embrace of knowledge-based recruitment and promotion heralds the rise of a meritocratic society where opportunities are earned based on one's capabilities rather than inherited privileges. This legacy of justice extends to every sector, every industry, and every institution, ensuring that individuals rise to positions of influence based on their merit, determination, and contributions.

A Vision of Empowerment. In our transformed nation, employment eligibility is not a matter of chance; it's a vision of empowerment. It's a vision that beckons citizens to equip themselves with knowledge, seek experiences that enrich their expertise, and boldly step forward to prove their proficiency. Through this vision, individuals become architects of their success, contributing their unique talents to the tapestry of our nation's growth.

A Future Forged by Competence. As we forge ahead, knowledge becomes the compass that guides us toward a future of unparalleled achievement. The echo of academic pursuit, the weight of experience, and the challenge of proficiency tests propel us toward a destiny where excellence reigns and competence is celebrated. In embracing knowledge as the sine qua non for recruitment and promotion, we empower our transformed nation with a skilled and visionary workforce equipped to steer our collective journey toward prosperity, innovation, and enduring success.

CHAPTER 24

PSYCHIATRIC CENTERS AND MICROFINANCE FOR SURVIVORS

24-1 Healing the Scars: Psychiatric Centers for Trauma Recovery

In the tapestry of our transformed nation, one thread stands out with undeniable significance—the need to heal the wounds inflicted by past atrocities. Mass killings, rapes, and other crimes have left deep emotional scars on countless individuals, haunting their lives and casting shadows on their hopes for a brighter future. To address this pain and offer a path toward recovery, we must establish specialized psychiatric centers dedicated to healing the victims' hearts and minds.

Centers of Hope and Healing:

These psychiatric centers will serve as healing sanctuaries where trauma survivors can find solace, support, and professional guidance. The pain carried by victims of mass violence is not merely physical; it is a psychological burden that can be just as crippling. These centers will provide a safe environment where individuals can confront their traumas, process their emotions, and embark on a healing journey.

Tailored Therapeutic Approaches:

Recovery from trauma is not a one-size-fits-all process. Everyone's journey is unique and shaped by their experiences, backgrounds, and strengths. The psychiatric centers will offer a range of therapeutic approaches, including individual counseling, group therapy, art therapy, and cognitive-behavioral techniques. These methods help survivors regain their sense of self, rebuild their emotional resilience, and find a path toward reclaiming their lives.

Addressing Intergenerational Trauma:

The scars of mass violence don't only affect the direct victims; they can also have a lasting impact on future generations. The psychiatric centers will also address intergenerational trauma, where the pain and anguish are passed down from one generation to another. By providing specialized counseling for families and children affected by the trauma of their parents and grandparents, we break the cycle of pain and pave the way for a more harmonious future.

Empowering Survivors:

Beyond the therapeutic interventions, these centers will empower survivors by equipping them with coping skills, resilience-building techniques, and tools to manage their emotional well-being. Workshops, seminars, and skill-building programs will allow survivors to navigate their lives with greater confidence and a renewed sense of purpose.

A Beacon of Compassion:

Establishing psychiatric centers for trauma recovery is not just a healthcare initiative but a declaration of compassion and solidarity. It sends a powerful message to survivors that their pain is acknowledged and that our transformed nation is committed to their healing. These centers will stand as tangible symbols of our commitment to nurturing the emotional well-being of every citizen, recognizing that true prosperity encompasses both physical and mental health.

A Testament to Transformation:

The existence of these psychiatric centers will serve as a testament to our nation's determination to heal, transform, and rise above the traumas of the past. Through these centers, we demonstrate our commitment to creating a society that values the well-being of every individual, regardless of their history or circumstances. As survivors embark on their recovery journey, they will be supported by a network of professionals, fellow survivors, and a nation that stands beside them in solidarity.

Dear citizens, establishing psychiatric centers for trauma recovery is crucial to healing the wounds that mar our collective history. Let us come together to create a transformed nation where empathy, support, and healing are the cornerstones of our society. By providing survivors with the resources to rebuild their lives, we contribute to a future where hope triumphs over pain and our nation thrives as a beacon of compassion and strength.

24-2 Empowering Resilience: Micro Financial Banks for Repatriates and Survivors

In the heart of our transformed nation, a profound commitment to empowering the most vulnerable among us stands as a guiding principle. Repatriates, widows, and orphans who have endured the weight of refuge and loss deserve our compassion and active support in rebuilding their lives. To facilitate their journey towards self-reliance and prosperity, we will establish micro-financial banks tailored to the needs of repatriates and survivors, providing them with the means to start small businesses and secure their future.

A Platform for Economic Empowerment:

Microfinance banks are more than just financial institutions; they are vehicles of empowerment that offer survivors the opportunity to break free from the cycle of dependency. Many widows and orphans have lost their families' primary breadwinners, leaving them vulnerable. Through these banks, we will empower them with the tools to regain control over their economic well-being, fostering a sense of agency and resilience.

Accessible Financial Services:

These micro-financial banks will be designed to cater to the unique needs of survivors. Accessible loan facilities, minimal interest rates, and flexible repayment terms will ensure survivors can launch their small businesses without excessive financial constraints. By offering tailored financial services, we aim to create an environment where economic growth becomes attainable for those who need it most.

Entrepreneurial Development:

Starting a small business requires more than just financial support; it demands knowledge, skills, and mentorship. The micro-financial banks will collaborate with educational institutions and experts in entrepreneurship to offer survivors comprehensive training programs. These programs will equip them with the skills necessary to successfully run their businesses, from managing finances to marketing strategies.

Fostering Community and Solidarity:

Establishing micro-financial banks isn't just about providing financial resources; it's also about creating a sense of community and support. Survivors will be able to connect with others who share similar experiences, forming networks offering emotional support and collaborative business opportunities. By fostering this spirit of unity, we amplify the impact of our efforts, creating a thriving ecosystem of resilience.

Empowering Widows and Orphans:

Widows and orphans are not defined solely by their losses; they possess untapped potential, aspirations, and dreams. The micro-financial banks acknowledge this potential and allow them to build a sustainable future for themselves and their families. By offering financial stability, these banks give widows and orphans the means to secure an education for their children, access healthcare, and uplift their communities.

A Legacy of Empowerment:

Establishing microfinance banks for survivors reflects our nation's commitment to empowerment, resilience, and inclusive growth. We are sowing the seeds of self-sufficiency and economic prosperity by creating a supportive ecosystem where survivors can turn their entrepreneurial dreams into reality. This legacy will echo through generations as survivors become inspirations to their children and communities, showcasing the transformative power of determination and opportunity.

Dear citizens, creating micro financial banks for survivors is a tangible step towards building a nation where every individual, regardless of their circumstances, has the chance to thrive. By investing in the economic empowerment of widows and orphans, we foster a sense of purpose, dignity, and hope that propels our transformed nation forward. Let us stand united in our commitment to uplift those who need it most, contributing to a society that thrives on the strength of its collective support and shared dreams.

CHAPTER 25

TRANSFORMING THE LAND

Nurturing a Paradise in Burundi SAHUTUGA

In the serene embrace of peace and unity, the citizens of Burundi SAHUTUGA stand as stewards of a transformed land—a canvas of potential awaiting the artistry of progress. As we tread the path toward the paradise of Africa, we recognize the need to cultivate and elevate essential sectors that will shape our collective destiny. This chapter illuminates our commitment to rejuvenating critical sectors, birthing a nation where prosperity, sustainability, and harmony intertwine seamlessly.

Agriculture and Livestock: Nourishing the Nation:

At the heart of our transformation lies the nurturing of our agricultural and livestock industries. The fertile soil that blankets our land is the foundation for our prosperity. By implementing sustainable and modern farming practices, we harness the bounty of our land to ensure food security for all citizens.

Identifying Export-Oriented Crops is also a catalyst for rapid economic growth. The key to financial success is identifying crops in demand in global markets due to their unique qualities, nutritional value, or cultural significance.

Investing in livestock programs empowers our farmers and revitalizes rural communities, forging a thriving landscape of self-sufficiency. A structured approach to affiliate livestock programs encapsulates the essence of empowerment, accountability, and sustainability. By coupling the distribution of high-quality cattle with the prerequisites of adequate land and comprehensive documentation, families are not merely recipients but active participants in their journey toward prosperity. This structured framework represents a profound commitment to transformation, fostering a nation where empowered families are the engines of progress and the embodiment of resilience.

Education as the Pillar of Progress:

Education emerges as a fundamental pillar in our quest to cultivate a paradise. Our commitment to nurturing young minds is unwavering. By reforming and elevating our education system, we provide the tools for our future architects, engineers, doctors, and leaders to rise. Through knowledge, critical thinking, and innovation, we equip our youth to carry forward the mantle of transformation, propelling our nation to new heights.

Clean Energy and Mining

Clean and sustainable energy sources will power our journey in our pursuit of transformation. With an emphasis on renewable energy technologies such as solar, wind, and hydroelectric power, we will reduce our carbon footprint and enhance our energy security. By embracing innovation and adopting environmentally friendly practices, we illuminate the path to a brighter, greener future for Burundi SAHUTUGA.

Precious treasures have been deposited in our land by the creator of the universe for all citizens. These natural resources —gold, nickel, rare earth, and more—represent geological wonders and symbols of our nation's potential and prosperity.

These resources beneath our soil are a source of both potential and responsibility. In the mining sector, we will strive for responsible and sustainable practices that benefit all our citizens and protect our environment.

Revitalizing Commerce and Infrastructure:

As the gears of progress turn, we rejuvenate our commerce and infrastructure sectors. We fortify our connection with the world by building modern transport networks, expanding airports, and enhancing port facilities. State-of-the-art marketplaces become bustling hubs, offering local and international products under one roof. This resurgence energizes trade, spurs economic activity, and amplifies opportunities for citizens and businesses.

The role of the diaspora in our nation's prosperity extends far beyond their lifetime. In the diaspora's investment lies the key to unlocking rapid economic growth. Their involvement in the management and ownership of businesses injects vitality into our economy, fostering innovation, creating job opportunities, and stimulating commerce. This catalytic effect transforms mere potential into tangible progress, propelling our transformed nation toward unparalleled prosperity.

Fostering Healthcare and Well-Being:

The well-being of our citizens is a cornerstone of our transformation. A robust healthcare system ensures that access to quality medical services is a fundamental right for all. By establishing well-equipped healthcare facilities and training programs, we cultivate a healthier nation, enabling individuals to participate in Burundi SAHUTUGA's prosperity fully.

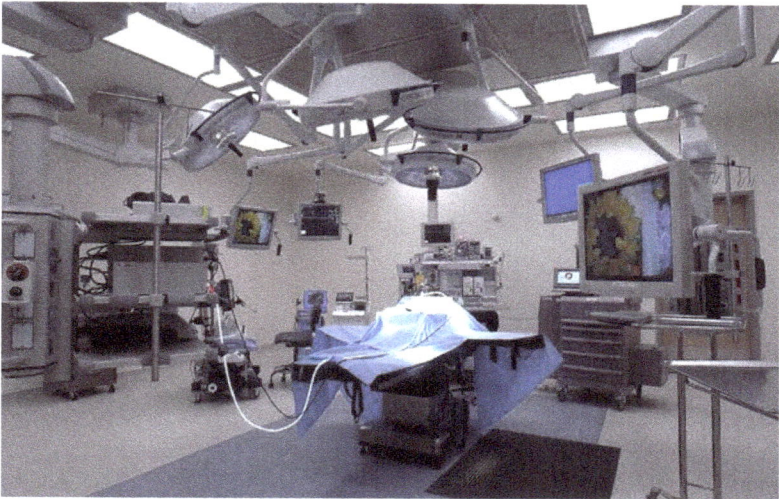

Building small water treatment plants in rural areas unveils a blueprint for community health. These plants harness advanced technology to purify water sources, ensuring that every drop that reaches households is free from contaminants. This strategy safeguards health and engenders a sense of security and confidence within communities.

Cultivating Tourism and Cultural Preservation:

Our paradise extends beyond the tangible—it encompasses our cultural heritage and the natural beauty surrounding us. We reimagine our tourism sector, enhancing and preserving the allure of our nation. By restoring historical sites, supporting local artisans, and showcasing our rich traditions, we beckon visitors to experience the tapestry of Burundi SAHUTUGA. In this place, nature's majesty and cultural treasures converge.

Continuous Growth: Our commitment to transformation extends beyond these sectors. While we prioritize these foundational areas, we are equally dedicated to continually evaluating and developing other industries that contribute to our nation's growth. A holistic approach is essential for our nation's prosperity, and we are unwavering in our dedication to realizing our vision.

Dear citizens, our plan is not a static blueprint but a dynamic roadmap that adapts to our nation's evolving needs and challenges. As architects of this transformation, we understand that the journey involves collective effort, collaboration, and continuous growth. Together, we are building a nation marked by unity, progress, and prosperity, a country that our citizens, present and future, will be proud to call their own.

CHAPTER 26

THE ESSENCE OF NATIONAL INDEPENDENCE

26-1 The Multifaceted Essence of National Independence
National independence is a multi-dimensional concept that goes far beyond administrative sovereignty. It encompasses the ideals of financial prosperity and individual freedoms that form the cornerstone of a thriving society. As we continue to shape our transformed nation, we recognize that true independence is a tapestry woven from economic strength, freedom of expression, and the power of the vote.

Economic Empowerment:
Financial prosperity is an integral component of national independence. A nation's ability to chart its economic course, develop its resources, and foster a vibrant business landscape

contributes to its self-sufficiency and resilience. In our transformed country, economic prosperity is not confined to a few; instead, it is a collective achievement that ensures a higher standard of living for all citizens. By investing in industries, education, and innovation, we lay the foundation for a strong and dynamic economy that empowers us on the global stage.

Freedom of Expression:

A nation thrives when its citizens freely express their thoughts, opinions, and ideas without fear. Freedom of expression is a cornerstone of democracy, allowing individuals to contribute to public discourse, challenge norms, and hold those in power accountable. In our transformed nation, our citizens' diverse voices will be valued and actively encouraged. This freedom creates an environment where innovation, progress, and creativity flourish, leading to an open-minded, adaptive, and resilient society.

Power of the Vote:

The power to cast a vote is the epitome of citizen empowerment. It embodies individual agency and is the driving force behind representative governance. Our transformed nation recognizes the significance of this power, and we are committed to ensuring that every citizen's voice is heard through fair and transparent elections. By participating in the democratic process, citizens become architects of their nation's destiny, steering its course toward the collective vision of prosperity, justice, and unity.

Harmonious Coexistence:

National independence is not a singular pursuit but a collective endeavor. It is a commitment to harmonious coexistence, where the rights and aspirations of every citizen are upheld. By nurturing a society where economic opportunities are accessible, freedom of expression is celebrated, and voting rights are safeguarded, we create an environment where everyone can thrive. This harmony is the essence of our transformed nation—a place where diversity is celebrated, and the collective strength of our people propels us forward.

Conclusion:

National independence is a tapestry woven from diverse threads—economic empowerment, freedom of expression, and the power of the vote. In our transformed nation, we recognize that true independence is achieved when citizens can prosper, voice their opinions, and contribute to shaping the nation's future. As we continue this transformative journey, let us remember that the road to true independence is paved with every citizen's aspirations, efforts, and dreams. Together, we will build a nation that stands as a testament to the unwavering pursuit of a brighter, more prosperous future for all.

26-2 Implementing New Strategies for Lasting Change

In the journey of transformation, the initial steps towards change may be exhilarating, but the actual test lies in sustaining the momentum over the long term. We must diligently implement new strategies, which act as pillars, supporting the foundation of lasting change and ensuring that the transformed society continues to progress toward a brighter future.

Education and Awareness: One of the fundamental strategies to sustain transformation is education and awareness. An informed and engaged citizenry is essential for upholding democratic values and supporting the principles of inclusivity and justice.

Education empowers citizens to understand the significance of their transformed identity and the historical context that led to the changes. By learning about the importance of reconciliation, empathy, and the pursuit of common goals, citizens become advocates for a cohesive and harmonious society.

Institutional Reforms: Sustainable change requires restructuring institutions to align with the new values and goals of the transformed society. Implementing institutional reforms ensures that the democratic system functions effectively and transparently and that the rights and aspirations of citizens are protected.

These reforms include strengthening accountability mechanisms, promoting merit-based appointments, and enhancing citizen engagement in decision-making processes. By creating institutions that reflect the transformed society's values, citizens gain trust in the system, reinforcing their commitment to the democratic journey.

Community Engagement: The support and involvement of communities are critical for sustaining transformation. Community engagement initiatives foster a sense of collective responsibility, encouraging citizens to actively contribute to developing their neighborhoods, towns, and cities.

These initiatives may include community forums, town hall meetings, and participatory planning processes. Engaging citizens at the grassroots level enables them to address local challenges and co-create solutions, leading to a stronger sense of ownership over the transformation.

Intergenerational Transfer of Values: To ensure the continuity of transformation, values such as empathy, inclusivity, and respect must be passed down through generations. Families, schools, and community organizations play a pivotal role in instilling these values in the younger members of society.

Intergenerational transfer of values fosters a sense of continuity, as future citizens inherit the legacy of positive change from their predecessors. By preserving and reinforcing the transformed identity and democratic ideals, society maintains its commitment to progress.

Continuous Evaluation and Adaptation: Sustaining transformation requires continuously evaluating progress and adapting strategies as needed. Monitoring the impact of implemented initiatives allows for informed decision-making and course correction when necessary.

Flexibility and responsiveness to changing circumstances ensure the transformation remains relevant and practical. This adaptive approach ensures that the society evolves with the times, staying attuned to the needs and aspirations of its citizens.

International Cooperation: Transformations are not isolated events but are part of a broader global context. International cooperation and partnerships can play a significant role in sustaining positive change.

Collaboration with other nations and international organizations can offer valuable insights and support for implementing best practices in governance, human rights, and sustainable development. By participating in global efforts toward positive change, the transformed society gains strength from the collective wisdom of the international community.

In conclusion, the sustainability of transformation relies on implementing new strategies that reinforce the changes in identity, family tree, nation's name, and the democratic system. Education and awareness, institutional reforms, community engagement, intergenerational value transfer, continuous evaluation, and international cooperation uphold lasting change.

As architects of our destiny, we recognize that sustaining transformation requires dedication and adaptability. By nurturing a society rooted in empathy, inclusivity, and justice, we pave the way for a future where positive change endures, empowering citizens to build a thriving and harmonious society for generations to come.

CHAPTER 27

THE SUPREME MONITORING BOARD: GUARDIANS OF TRANSFORMATION

Adaptability and responsiveness are paramount in the dynamic journey of transforming our nation. As we steer our ship through the uncharted waters of progress, we must have a steady hand to navigate challenges, address issues, and ensure continued alignment with our transformational vision. To fulfill this crucial role, we introduce the concept of the Supreme Monitoring Board. This body is the sentinel of our nation's transformation, vigilant and empowered to guide us through every phase.

Establishing the Supreme Monitoring Board:

The Supreme Monitoring Board is not just an administrative entity but a cornerstone of our commitment to a transparent, accountable, and efficient transformation process. Comprising individuals of impeccable integrity, expertise, and dedication, this board is entrusted with overseeing the implementation of our transformation initiatives. Its members are drawn from diverse fields, encompassing economics, governance, social welfare, environment, and more. Their collective wisdom ensures a holistic approach to addressing challenges and seizing opportunities.

Roles and Responsibilities:

1. **Oversight and Evaluation:** The primary function of the Supreme Monitoring Board is to oversee the execution of our transformational plans. Regular evaluations are conducted to assess progress, identify blockages, and recommend corrective measures. This proactive approach ensures that our journey remains on course, even in the face of unexpected hurdles.

2. **Issue Resolution:** Challenges are inherent to any transformational journey. The board acts as a rapid-response team capable of swiftly addressing emerging issues. By analyzing challenges and proposing solutions, they prevent roadblocks from impeding our progress.

3. **Policy and Strategy Development:** The board collaborates with experts to develop comprehensive policies and strategies that drive our transformation forward. These strategic initiatives are grounded in data, research, and the collective vision of our nation.

4. **Transparency and Accountability:** Transparency is the bedrock of our transformational journey. The board ensures that all actions are transparent and accountable, enhancing public trust and participation in our journey.

5. **Adaptation and Innovation:** Our nation's landscape and strategies are evolving. The board is at the forefront of identifying opportunities for innovation and transformation, keeping our approach fresh, relevant, and responsive to changing circumstances.

Working in Unity:

The Supreme Monitoring Board operates as a cohesive unit, collaborating with various sectors, government bodies, and private entities. Its effectiveness lies in bridging gaps, facilitating communication, and fostering collaboration among stakeholders. By uniting our efforts, we harness the collective intelligence of our nation to overcome challenges and maximize opportunities.

A Legacy of Excellence:

As we march forward, it is imperative to ensure that the legacy of our transformation is one of excellence, integrity, and prosperity. The Supreme Monitoring Board is not a mere formality but a testament to our commitment to excellence in governance, strategy, and execution. By entrusting this board with the responsibility of safeguarding our transformation, we secure a legacy that future generations will inherit with pride.

Dear citizens, the Supreme Monitoring Board is not just an administrative body—it is a custodian of our dreams, a guardian of our progress, and a partner in our journey towards a transformed and prosperous nation. With the board's guidance, vigilance, and dedication, we stand ready to overcome any challenges, adapt to any circumstance, and create a legacy that inspires future generations.

CHAPTER 28

A VISION UNVEILED

A vision for a nation is a clear and inspiring picture of what the country aspires to become in the future. It outlines the collective goals, values, and ambitions that guide the nation's development and progress. This vision often encompasses ideals like peace, prosperity, unity, and social harmony, serving as a roadmap for both short-term and long-term objectives. It provides a sense of purpose and direction, motivating citizens and leaders to work together to achieve a better future for all.

The Radiance of Burundi SAHUTUGA

In the tapestry of our transformed nation Burundi SAHUTUGA, the present and future generations shall witness a landscape adorned with the marks of progress and prosperity. As the sun rises over our horizons, it illuminates a world where the dreams of unity, democracy, and national integrity have blossomed into reality. From the quaint corners of our small towns to the bustling heart of our cities, the vision of Burundi SAHUTUGA emerges in vibrant detail.

Modern Infrastructure: A Testament to Progress

Our transformed nation boasts modern infrastructure that criss-crosses our land. Paved roads stretch like lifelines, connecting communities and enabling the seamless flow of goods and services. Bridges span rivers and valleys, bridging physical gaps and metaphorical divides. High-tech communication networks weave us into a global tapestry, ensuring that we are connected, informed, and empowered.

A Symphony of Small Towns: The Heartbeat of Unity

Picture small towns nestled amidst the rolling hills, where the echoes of laughter and camaraderie fill the air. Each city, a microcosm of unity, celebrates the spirit of diversity as residents from various backgrounds harmonize to build a shared destiny. Adorned with names that honor our heroes, the streets testify to the sacrifices made to forge a united nation.

Urban Marvels: Cities of Prosperity and Progress

As the sun reaches its zenith, it casts a warm glow upon the cities of Burundi SAHUTUGA. Skyscrapers reach for the sky, their architectural brilliance a testament to human ingenuity. The town centers buzz with activity, markets brimming with local produce, crafts, and innovations. Clean and efficient public transportation networks crisscross the urban landscapes, connecting people and opportunities.

Educational Hubs and Technological Marvels: Nurturing Minds, Shaping Futures

Our journey takes us through educational hubs that nurture the minds of the present and future generations. Universities and schools are beacons of knowledge, cultivating thinkers, innovators, and leaders. Technological marvels punctuate the landscape, emphasizing our embrace of progress. These centers of learning and innovation propel our nation forward on the global stage.

Sustainable Agriculture: Nourishing Our Future

As we traverse the fertile lands of Burundi SAHUTUGA, we witness sustainable agriculture practices that yield bountiful harvests. Fields are adorned with crops nurtured through modern techniques and traditional wisdom. Fruit plantations stretch as far as the eye can see, promising a future where food security is assured and the land is respected as a source of sustenance.

New Horizons: Airports and Aircrafts

As we traverse the expanse of our nation, we encounter a network of modern airports—a testament to our commitment to efficient transportation. Aircraft taxis grace the skies, carrying passengers to various corners of our transformed land and bordering countries. These cutting-edge innovations represent our dedication to conscious solutions, paving the way for sustainable travel and connectivity.

Renovated Tourist Sites: Unveiling the Beauty of Our Land

As we explore our transformed nation, we stumble upon renovated tourist sites that showcase the natural beauty and cultural heritage of Burundi SAHUTUGA. The Kibira National Park invites us to connect with nature's splendor, while the Rusizi National Park and the Ruvubu National Park let us witness the harmony between wildlife and humanity. National museums and monuments echo the stories of our past, enriching our present and enlightening the future.

A Technological Marvel: Digital Connectivity

In the digital age, our transformed nation harnesses the power of technology to connect citizens and empower communities. Broadband networks crisscross the country, ensuring every corner of Burundi SAHUTUGA is digitally connected. Online platforms streamline government services, education, and commerce, fostering efficiency and accessibility.

Innovative Infrastructure and Sustainable Technologies: A Green Horizon

In our transformed nation, innovative infrastructure and sustainable technologies define our progress. Solar panels glint atop rooftops, wind turbines sway in harmony with the breeze, and eco-friendly transportation networks crisscross the land. These visible symbols of our commitment to a greener future inspire hope and pave the way for future generations.

Cultural and Historical Treasures: Museums and Monuments

Our transformed nation proudly celebrates its rich history and culture through museums and monuments. The National Museum houses artifacts that narrate our journey from the past to the present, and the Geological Museum showcases the wonders of our land. Monuments dedicated to unity, democracy, and national integrity stand as beacons of inspiration, reminding us of the ideals we hold dear.

Economic Empowerment: Thriving Markets and Industries

Burundi SAHUTUGA's economic landscape blooms with a diversity of industries. Modern markets hum with activities, offering many local and international products. Manufacturing companies produce goods that reflect our innovation and craftsmanship, while microfinance banks specializing in livestock affiliate programs empower farmers to cultivate success.

Conclusion: A Radiant Vision

In the vibrant mosaic of Burundi SAHUTUGA, the present and future generations behold a nation that has undergone a remarkable transformation. From the smallest town to the grandest city, from the skies above to the ground beneath, every element bears the mark of progress, unity, and promise. Our vision for Burundi SAHUTUGA shines brightly, a testament to the dedication and efforts of every citizen, past and present, who has contributed to our transformation journey.

A CHOICE FOR THE FUTURE

Dear Fellow Citizens,

As we stand at the threshold of a new chapter in our nation's history, we reflect on the journey we have collectively undertaken—a journey of transformation, unity, and progress. We have diligently sown the seeds of change, nurturing them with our unwavering dedication and shared vision. The four unbendable pillars we raise are a testament to our commitment to unity, justice, prosperity, and compassion.

The path before us is a crossroads—a choice that demands our attention and deliberation. It is a choice that asks us to consider the lessons of our past, our present aspirations, and our future generations' dreams. We are faced with a decision that will shape the destiny of our nation for years to come—a decision that carries the weight of responsibility and the promise of hope.On the one hand, we can choose to continue the faulty foundation of division and conflict—a path that has haunted us for far too long. We can allow history to repeat itself, perpetuating the cycles of mistrust, hatred, and suffering that marred our past. We can ignore the pain of our ancestors, our heroes' sacrifices, and our youth's potential—a future characterized by a legacy of missed opportunities and shattered dreams.

On the other hand, we have the undeniable choice to embrace the legacy we have painstakingly built—a legacy that beckons us toward unity, harmony, and progress. We can honor the sacrifices of those who came before us by standing firm on the foundation of our transformed nation. We can heed the call of our youth, who yearn for a future unburdened by the mistakes of the past. We can decide to be the architects of change, the bearers of hope, and the champions of a better tomorrow—a legacy that our future generations will be proud to inherit.

Dear fellow citizens, the power to decide the course of our nation's destiny rests in our hands. It is a choice that transcends political affiliations, regional differences, and individual ambitions. It is a choice that unites us in purpose and ignites the spark of collective action. As architects of this transformation, we have built the framework for a future that defies the limitations of history—a future where unity, justice, prosperity, and compassion reign.

Let us not falter at this pivotal moment. Let us rise above the divisions that have held us back, the prejudices that have torn us apart, and the wounds that have scarred us. Let us stand united, shoulder to shoulder, hand in hand, and heart to heart. Let us choose the path that leads to a transformed nation—a nation that stands as a beacon of hope, an example of progress, and a legacy of unity.

The choice is ours, dear citizens. It is a choice to define our future, to honor our past, and to create a legacy that resonates through generations. Let us make the decision that will make our future generations proud of us. This decision paves the way for a transformed nation where prosperity, peace, and unity flourish.

With unwavering resolve,

Audace Mpoziriniga
Chief Architect of a Transformed Nation
Burundi SAHUTUGA

SUMMARY

In the grand tapestry of history, nations have risen and fallen, societies have evolved, and people have striven for unity, purpose, and prosperity. In the heart of Africa, a country embarks on a journey of transformation, reconciliation, and renewal. At the heart of this journey is a word that carries profound meaning. This word can illuminate an entire country, strengthen its economy, and lay a foundation for future generations to thrive. That word is "SAHUTUGA."

SAHUTUGA is not just a word; it is a beacon of hope, a symbol of unity, and a testament to the indomitable spirit of a nation that emerges from the shadows of division and conflict. It is a word that resonates in the hearts and minds of every citizen of Burundi SAHUTUGA, reminding them of the power of transformation.

In a land where historical divisions once threatened to tear the nation asunder, SAHUTUGA arrives like a clap of thunder, piercing through the darkness of division and illuminating the path toward unity and reconciliation. It is a word that carries the weight of history, the aspirations of the present, and the promise of a brighter future.

Just as the seasons change, so does Burundi enter a new season of unity, of coming together as one people, bound not by past divisions but by a shared vision of prosperity, peace, and progress. SAHUTUGA represents the end of an era marked by strife and discord and the beginning of a new era where the people of this nation stand united, hand in hand, ready to face the challenges and opportunities that lie ahead.

Every nation has its defining moments, its pivotal historical junctures, when it must choose the path it wishes to follow. For Burundi SAHUTUGA, that moment has arrived with the introduction of this powerful word. SAHUTUGA is more than just a linguistic novelty; it is a clarion call for transformation. It symbolizes the collective will of a nation to break free from the shackles of division, to heal the wounds of the past, and to forge a future where unity, inclusivity, and love prevail.

As SAHUTUGA takes root in the collective consciousness of Burundi SAHUTUGA's citizens, it becomes more than a word; it becomes a living testament to the resilience and determination of a nation. SAHUTUGA embodies a new beginning, a fresh start, and a chance to build a society where every citizen can thrive regardless of background, region, or beliefs.

One word can indeed change the course of a nation's history, and SAHUTUGA is that word for Burundi SAHUTUGA. It is a word that reminds us that even in the face of adversity, we have the power to transform, to heal, and to unite.

SAHUTUGA is our foundation guiding star, sparkling unity, love, and prosperity to future generations.

As we journey forward, let us remember the significance of this word and let it serve as a constant reminder of our shared commitment to a brighter future. With SAHUTUGA as our guiding light, there is no challenge too great, no division too deep, and no obstacle too daunting. We are Burundian SAHUTUGA, united in purpose and bound by the promise of a transformed and prosperous nation.

SAHUTUGA—the word that brings unity, the word that ignites hope, the word that will illuminate our path towards a paradise called Burundi SAHUTUGA.

ABOUT THE AUTHOR

Audace Mpoziriniga: Architect of Unity and Transformation

Audace Mpoziriniga, born in February and identifying as a Hutu according to the SAHUTUGA approach, is the visionary architect of unity and transformation of Burundi SAHUTUGA. He is a family man with four daughters and three sons, devoted to one woman, with a deep understanding of the complexities of family life. His upbringing, a blend of rural and urban experiences, enriched his insights into the diverse fabric of Burundi SAHUTUGA.

Audace as an independent researcher and thinker always had a burning desire to eradicate suffering among the innocent population caught in the crossfire of political conflicts. His critical thinking and analytical skills led him to explore the nation's political framework, ultimately giving birth to the SAHUTUGA concept.

SAHUTUGA is not just a word; it's a symbol of unity and transformation that Audace envisions for his nation. It represents an end to division and the beginning of an era where peace, democracy, and prosperity thrive. Audace's mission is to provide a strong foundation for lasting peace and genuine democracy, healing the wounds of the past and uniting the people of Burundi SAHUTUGA.

Audace invites all to join him in this extraordinary journey that transcends divisions and embraces the promise of a united and prosperous Burundi SAHUTUGA.

www.ingramcontent.com/pod-product-compliance
Lightning Source LLC
Chambersburg PA
CBHW051244020426
42333CB00025B/3047